Volume 8
English

*Trade Secrets of a
    Haircolor Expert*

Presents

Coloring African-American, Natural and Chemically Relaxed Hair

TCC South

Crowley Learning Center

David Velasco & Paul Chambers

Coloring African American Natural and Chemically Relaxed Hair

Disclaimer

This course is designed to educate and inform its readers of the subject matter covered herein. The publisher and author do not warrant any guarantee or responsibility to any person or entity with respect to any loss or damage caused directly or indirectly by the information contained in this book. The reader is expressly warned to consider and adopt all safety precautions that might be indicated by the activities herein and to avoid all potential hazards. By following the instructions contained herein, the reader willingly assumes all risk and liability in connection with such instructions.

Other Haircolor Education Programs From David Velasco

HaircolorTradeSecrets.com
FREE Haircolor Ebook
Haircolor Books - Creative Foiling DVD's - Audio CD's
Trade Secrets of a Haircolor Expert
David Velasco

HaircolorClubhouse.com
FREE Haircolor VIDEOS
Network with Thousands of Hairdressers - Haircolor BLOGS - Haircolor Photos
The Haircolor Experts "Networking Club House"
by David Velasco

HaircolorUniversity.com
12 Month - MultiMedia E-Course in the Art of Haircolor
Streaming and Downloadable - Videos - Audios - PDF
Haircolor University
By David Velasco

Copyright © 2013-2014. All Rights Reserved. Salon Success Systems

No part of this course may be reproduced or transmitted in any form or by any means, electronic or mechanical, including photocopying, recording or by any information storage and retrieval system without written permission from the authors, except for the inclusion of brief quotation in a review. Images in this course are a combination of original photography by David Velasco Salon, Ltd., computer generated illustrations and stock photography from a variety of resources. Permission request for reprints may be submitted in writing to Publisher: Salon Success Systems, 150 South Main Street, Doylestown, PA. 18901

Coloring African American Natural and Chemically Relaxed Hair

WHAT INDUSTRY LEADERS ARE SAYING ABOUT "TRADE SECRETS"

In the early 1990s, I made this decision to switch to Wella Hair exclusively for the Bumble and bumble salon. As we had been using a mixture of 4/5 hair color brands, this was an extremely difficult transition. At that time, we had nine colorists and we were one of the busiest salons in New York. The first week of transition was extremely difficult with everyone completely confused and the results were varied.

It was at this point that I first met David Velasco. He had just finished a long stint as the art director and head colorist for Wella US and he very much wanted to come work at Bumble. I hired him specifically to try and help us make sense of this new color methodology that we were going to be using. With David's help, things changed and improved almost immediately. Apart from his quiet leadership and charismatic way, he was simply never ruffled. Further, he has a very deep understanding of the basic concepts of hair color as well as the complex tasks that some clients choose to do. He managed very quickly to make sure that all nine colorists were confident in the new haircolor and made sure they continued to broaden the skills and knowledge that they were missing and strengthen their techniques. His overall personality and experience were huge boosts to a salon that had over 120 employees.

After five years, David decided to return to his own salon. However, he had made an indelible mark on the quality of work that our hair color department was able to produce. I would say that every salon in America should have this book series. It is a must read, must know, must study book.

Michael A. Gordon
Founder
Bumble and bumble

David
When you told me that you were writing a book I knew that it would be good, but what you wrote is the encyclopedia of haircolor!

Dee Levin
Salon Nornandee
Secretary of Intercoiffure-America

Coloring African American Natural and Chemically Relaxed Hair

Dear David,

I was reading your book again tonight. I must say, you have some INCREDIBLE CONTENT! You have a FABULOUS OPPORTUNITY to set a higher tone for haircolor education.

I think this book could set a new standard for "Non-manufacturer" education. You have done an EXQUISITE job writing a truly definitive work.
Again, your content is PHENOMENAL!
Wishing you all the very best! Stay in touch, -- you are on to something very special. This shows what a wonderful teacher you are.

Beth!

Beth Minardi

David,

I have just finished the first four chapters of your book and I must tell you that it is one of the best haircolor books I have ever seen.

One of the easiest to follow, great comments on the 'trade secrets', non commercial, and it is very obvious that you have a lot of knowledge and experience on haircolor from being behind the chair.

I look forward to reading the rest of the book and to seeing you in September

Fondly,
Sheila

Sheila Zaricor
Treasurer - International Haircolor Exchange

What You Will Learn in this Book   Pg.

- Introduction ---1
- An Overview of the Coloring Process --3
- Rules of Texture and Porosity ---9
- Understanding the pH Scale ---12
- The Theory of Haircolor Does Not Change---------------------------------------16
- 10 Most Important Laws of Haircolor--17
- Gray Coverage Rules Do Not Change---31
- The 5 Variables of Coloring African-American Hair----------------------------38
- Variable #1--THE HAIR'S NATURAL COLOR---------------------------------39
- Variable #2--2 KINDS OF TEXTURE --42
- Variable #3--3 TYPES OF NATURAL TEXTURE-----------------------------45
- Variable #4--5 STAGES OF POROSITY--52
- Variable #5--3 TYPES of CHEMICAL RELAXERS----------------------------60
- The Differences Between Ammonium Thiogylcolate and Hydroxide Relaxers --62
- Three Strengths of Hydroxide Relaxers Mild, Regular & Super ------------69
- pH of Chemical Relaxers--70
- Pre-treating Chemically Relaxed Hair for Color-------------------------------71
- Understanding the Formulation Charts ---75
- Haircolor Selector Grids and Hair Classification Charts----------------------78
- Group 1 – Natural Curl Texture Charts--85
- Group 2 – Chemically Relaxed Texture Charts-------------------------------101
- After Care ---- Hair Care Products --117
- After Care Retailing ---122
- At Home After-Care Maintenance Tips --124

Meet The Authors

David Velasco

David Velasco has been a haircolor specialist and educator for nearly 40 years, He is the Creator of:
Trade Secrets of a Haircolor Expert Educational Series

David has formally held positions as the National Artistic Director for the Wella Corporation, Haircolor Director for the Bumble & bumble Salon in New York City and presently owns his own color-specialty salon in Pennsylvania.

You can join him online at his haircolor forum: HaircolorClubhouse.com

Paul Chambers

Motivating. Inspiring and passionate are just a few words that describes Paul Chambers.

Paul is owner of *Paul Chambers Salon* located in theatre and art district of the south loop, of Chicago Illinois. His work has been featured in both in national print and media as a Multicultural Colorist and Master Cutter. Paul is also an Educator and a American Board Certified Colorist who travels throughout the United States teaching salon Professional's and beauty school students the art of coloring and cutting multi-ethnic hair.

Coloring African American Natural and Chemically Relaxed Hair

Introduction

As publisher and creator of the *Trade Secrets of a Haircolor Expert* Educational Series, it brings me great pleasure to introduce you to this new, **GROUND BREAKING** book.

This book is designed to not only teach you how to *color natural and chemically relaxed African American hair,* but also as a **reference book** which you will keep by your side at the salon on a daily basis.

This is the first book in the *HaircolorTrade Secrets Series* in which I have asked fellow haircolor expert, **Mr. Paul Chambers**, to co-author with me. My purpose for doing so is that I feel that no one can be an expert at everything (not even me :-/).

In my opinion in order to become an expert at something, one must do it every day, all day long, for a long time. This is the kind of expertise that Paul brings to the party.

I spent several years looking for just the right person to co-write this book with me and my perseverance paid off. Paul has a wealth of knowledge in this area and he also shares a passion for teaching it as I do. I simply could not have asked for a better partner in the creation of this incredible book.

Why I wanted to write this book

After writing my other books in the *Haircolor Trade Secrets Series*, there was a glaring omission, the African-American client! Not that I purposely neglected this topic, but as I said already, I did not feel that I was an expert at it.

However, I truly felt there was a strong need for better haircolor education on this topic due to the challenging nature of working with this very fragile and delicate hair type. Also, due to the fact that many times when working with African American clients, you will be working on hair that has been "chemically relaxed", which just adds to the complexities of the process.

It is my hope that this book will give you the tools you need to understand this complex specialty and to build your confidence in performing these services.

As always, we are here to help you any way we can.

David Velasco
Co-Author / Publisher

An Overview of the Coloring Process

The Consultation

Communication with a potential client begins the moment she calls for an appointment, or when she walks in the salon. Your guest is the most important asset in your business! It is the foundation for performing successful services.

The consultation establishes communication between the client and the stylist and gives you a clear direction for the desired look. The client's expectations can be set during this session, and the hair colorist can determine which method, products and services are needed.

In addition, clients get the perfect opportunity to explain their likes and dislikes about their hair and previous services. However, some clients can be more reserved or vague in giving you information about their hair history.

The more information you receive from the client by asking open ended questions, the better you are able to evaluate and deliver the color result that the client will be pleased with.

This is when your listening skills come to the forefront for clues and ideas each client expresses so that you don't miss any important information.

During the Consultation:

It is important to have the client to divulge all necessary hair history, at home regimens, products used and treatments used by the client. Leaving out key information can cause less than desired results.

Allergies and medications should also be shared so the colorist can take extra precaution when selecting and applying products. This knowledge removes the guesswork for the colorist in assessing the condition, hair type and client preferences BEFORE PERFORMING THE SERVICE OR USING THE PRODUCT OF CHOICE.

Coloring African American Natural and Chemically Relaxed Hair

We can't discuss change without first knowing what we are changing.

We first want to identify whether the hair:

- Is natural
- Is relaxed
- Is transitioning from relaxed hair
- Had previous chemical services
- Had sodium relaxers used
- Had no-lye relaxers used
- Is dark semi-permanent color or henna

Other considerations:

- Strength of any relaxer (mild, normal, super)
- Determine texture (fine, normal, coarse)
- Determine the *OTHER* kind of texture (Formation = wavy, curly, kinky)
- Determine density (thick, normal, sparse)
- Assess scalp issues (dry, normal, oily)
- Assess problematic issues (breakage, shedding, flaking, itching)
- Assess medications that has side effects that can cause hair thinning and/or hair loss
- Determine use of hair extensions (weaves, kinky twists, braids, etc.)
- Determine what is their preferred hairstyle?

These are the core questions you will need to ask before you provide any color or relaxer service. Once the hair is has been analyze, and after further discussion with the client, then you can advise her accordingly to make the right choices.

Key Note: When asking the client about her prior chemical service, you should ask:

- *What Type of relaxer (Lye or No Lye) was used?*
- *And what Strength relaxer (mild, normal, super)?*

If she doesn't remember (which is usually the case) what type of relaxer was used, you should ask if she has a sensitive scalp?

Then follow up with: was the relaxer mixed with an activator from a small container or was it taken from a large relaxer bucket?

Note: if the relaxer was mix from a small container with activator than it is usually a calcium relaxer. If it comes directly from the 4lb relaxer tub than its usually sodium relaxer.

Coloring African American Natural and Chemically Relaxed Hair

This at least gives you a clue as to if the relaxer is sodium (Lye) or a sensitive scalp relaxer (No-Lye). This will give clues as to what you will be working before you offer her the service she has been wanting. Remember if the hair isn't in good condition healthier choices should be considered –for example using a no lift deposit only demi –permanent which has a lower level ph balance then permanent color or use a semi color which has no developer. Of course, always suggest and offer a deep conditioning treatment for the client.

One last thing: If the client tells you her strength of relaxer was sodium regular or super strength , we strongly suggest that you **do not proceed into permanent or lightening service until you bring her pH balance under control**.

You can do this by giving the client a moisture protein treatment (we will cover this later) so that the cuticle and elasticity will not be compromised, when she gets her color service. **This is a very crucial juncture, of the consultation.**

It will be a deciding factor if she should have a non-oxidative color as oppose to permanent color. Better to be safe than sorry!

Formulating Client Preferences:

Using as many visual aids as possible are recommended to communicate and express what is on the client's mind. It also gives you a powerful resource to show your client what will suit her. Words like honey blonde, cherry red, and champagne blonde could paint two very different pictures in your mind versus your client's mind. It's much better to **show** her the color, so it can be seen!

Remember a picture is worth 1000 words!

Coloring African American Natural and Chemically Relaxed Hair

What's the Natural Level of The Hair?

Knowing the natural base level is the foundation before formulating color. Remember that permanent color can only lighten so much. We call this:

"The Limitations of a Tint"

Most African Americans primarily have dark to medium brown hair, which usually stays the same until gray begins to take over. By identifying the natural level, which is usually between levels 2 to 3 for most African Americans, this will help you to determine the limits of lightness that the permanent color can achieve.

Most African-Americans have medium to dark brown natural hair color
This is the only constant that we have in the equation

IF the client wants to be lighter than she already is, and you know that you will not be able to get her as light as she want to be with a tint, then you should explain to her exactly what is possible and what is not and that you may have to use a lightener (bleach product) to get her to the degree of lightness she wants to be.

There are three universal possible variations of natural color:

1. Lighter
2. Darker
3. Different tone

It's the colorist's responsibility to find out what is the clients natural level. Ask her about her own color and what color and tone she would like to be. Then just listen for the important details. (This involves active listening, don't wander). Once she is finished, the colorist should begin to give feedback and advice. The feedback given should be defined by:

- Her skin tone and eye color
- Her personality, lifestyle and profession
- Her haircut and hairstyle

Coloring African American Natural and Chemically Relaxed Hair

Universal Laws of Formulating
After you have gone through the consultation process and have extracted as much information to qualify the client for the service by asking, listening and visually assessing the condition of the hair, Then your are on your way to formulating the color to get the desired end result for your client.

The steps you take to arrive at the end result are:

Natural Base Level + Artificial Color or lightener + Developer + Contributing Color Pigment = Final Result

- Starting tone -- natural color
- Desired level -- 1 thru 10 level of lightness
- Desired tone -- warm, cool or neutral

NOTE: This is where pictures help you and the client arrive at same color tone before you formulate. Describing color is non -productive without pictures.

- Percentage of gray – 10%, 25%, 50% or more
- Texture of hair – fine, medium or coarse
- Stage of Porosity – 1.) New growth 2.) Midshaft 3.) Ends

Coloring African American Natural and Chemically Relaxed Hair

> **Haircolor Secret**
>
> When hair is overly porous, lower the volume of peroxide and incorporate warm tones in your formula to avoid dark non-reflective color.

Your desired tone will be the determining factor in assisting you in choosing your color product, Semi-Permanent, Demi- Permanent or lightener.

When using a lightener (bleach) or permanent hair color on **dark pigmented relaxed hair, make sure the client's hair was previously relaxed with a <u>MILD</u> strength relaxer.**

I strongly recommend that you never color someone's hair on the same day that you do a relaxer or any other chemical service, no matter what anyone or any manufacturer tells you. Remember it's about thinking long-term (career) not short term (a hustle) maintaining The structural integrity of the hair and trust of your client is the utmost importance in building a solid color clientele.

Summary:

- You can't always tell if a client's hair is weak just by looking at it. Make sure to ask your clients about the last time they had a color or chemical service and take the time to consult with your client about her desired results.

- With all clients including African American clients, the consultation needs to begin with a discussion of the hair's condition before any chemical service is suggested or applied.

- A Relaxer client's hair will generally start at a more porous degree than natural hair.

- Finding out what **type of relaxer** and **strength of relaxer** or **at home product** was used is paramount before deciding what color product or formula to use.

- Deciding what formula you are going to use is not exactly formulating color, instead formulation is deciding which levels and tone you will use to get the desired end result. You will always have to consider the condition of the hair you are about to color.

- The rules of formulation are the same for everyone; however, when working with African American hair, porosity (condition of hair) is of great concern

NOTE: I would recommend using no higher that 20 –volume developer when using a permanent hair color on relaxed hair. And use 10 vol developer when highlighting on relaxed hair. However if the hair is virgin, dense, coarse and is in good condition you can use 25 volume for Permanent Color Use Only.

Refer to your abbreviation section it will show you how to create 25vol for your dispensary.

Coloring African American Natural and Chemically Relaxed Hair

The First and Most Important Rule in Coloring African-American Hair is Understanding the In-Depth
Rules of Texture and Porosity

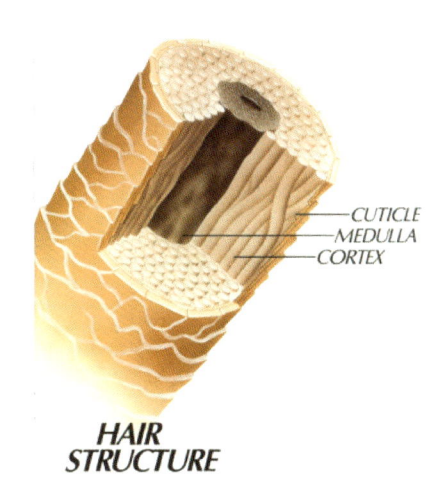

What is Hair?

Hair is actually a nonliving fiber made from a protein called keratin. Keratin, in turn, is made up of long chains of amino acids created from 5 elements: carbon, oxygen, hydrogen, nitrogen and sulfur. These chains are linked together like a bicycle chain and are also cross-linked together by what are known as **side bonds**.

These bonds are responsible for the strength and elasticity of the hair strand. Each hair strand is made up of three parts: the cuticle, the cortex and the medulla. The medulla is the innermost layer of the hair; however, not everyone has one and it is most commonly found only in thick, coarse hair. It is the cuticle and cortex we need to be most concerned with as it pertains to the overall integrity of the hair.

The Cuticle
The cuticle is the outer layer of hair. It is not one solid layer, it is made of individual scales that lay against one another just like closed blinds. The cuticle of a healthy hair strand will lie flat and protect the inside of the hair shaft against damage, as well as keep moisture in your hair where it belongs. Learning how to keep the cuticle layer closed is directly related to using products that control and maintain the pH balance. This is one of the major keys in keeping the hair in great condition.

The Cortex
The cortex is the middle layer of the hair shaft. The cortex itself is responsible for approximately 90 percent of your hair's total weight; additionally, the natural color of your hair is determined within the cortex by a pigment known as melanin. The permanent chemical changes that takes place in the hair shaft that are caused by relaxers, perms, texturizing and permanent haircolor, takes place within the cortex.

Coloring African American Natural and Chemically Relaxed Hair

Hair Texture is Everything:

Once we know what texture we are working on, then we can focus on how to arrive at the final outcome we envision for our clients.

Two Kinds of Hair Texture

The word **texture** has two different meanings when working on African-American hair.

The traditional meaning of hair texture is **the diameter of each hair strand (fine, medium and course)** and that does indeed still play a role in working with African-American hair, of course, African-American hair does fall into the same 3-texture categories.

However, in the world of coloring African-American hair the word texture also means, or stands for, the **texture of the curl pattern (formation), which a client may have.**

1. Wavy
2. Curly
3. Kinky

To sum this up, the defining nature of texture is measured by the degree of fineness to coarseness of the hair, which varies according to the diameter of each individual hair. As different fabrics respond differently to dyeing, various hair textures react differently to haircolor and relaxers differently.

This is important because the physical structure (chemically relaxed hair or previous colored hair) will affect the final outcome of the color formula. It's formulating the right color for the appropriate texture and porosity level of the client's hair.

The diverse range of hair textures (formations) among African American clients from a natural tighter curl to looser waves to straight chemically relaxed hair varies according to different ethnic backgrounds within the culture. This makes the process of creating beautiful haircolor challenging when your want to keep hair in a healthy condition. However, by identifying the texture you are working with your will bring into view what products, tools and chemicals, you should choose for the client you are servicing.

Within each category of *"formation texture"* **(wavy, curly, kinky)** you also need to evaluate if the *"diameter texture"* is **fine, normal or coarse.**

The categories of texture are standard regardless of ethnicity. When we mention texture in our everyday conversation, we are referring to hair that is not smooth or straight. However, that is insufficient when deciding what product or color service is needed for a particular client. We have to apply the defining universal characteristics of determining if the texture is fine, medium, or coarse (naturally kinky or curly) to get a more complete picture.

I know all this talk about the two types of texture may sound a little confusing, but hang in there and it will all make better sense as we move along.

Coloring African American Natural and Chemically Relaxed Hair

Fine hair texture is often simpler to process, easier to lift, quicker to fade and can be over-processed easily. Fine hair has a thinner cortex and often no medulla. It is also very small in diameter and tends to be oily and weightless.

Flyaway hair is most often associated with people who have fine hair. You'll find if you do have fine hair, it will not hold a curl easily and it's often limp with no body.

Fine Hair:

- Doesn't hold styles well
- Can become weighed down with heavy products, causing the hair to look stringy
- Can look thin
- Can break easily, because it's fragile

Medium or Average Hair:

Is the most common type of texture in both men and women. It doesn't require any special considerations for chemical services and usually processes normally. Medium texture has the flexibility to take on wider range of ingredients and products. It has the most styling flexibility of all three-hair types.

- Holds styles fairly well
- Usually looks thick and covers the scalp well
- Is not as prone to breakage as fine hair
- Needs no special considerations in chemical processing
- Allows for a broader range in product usage

Coarse Hair:

Coarse hair has a much thicker cortex and structurally stronger than other hair textures. This hair texture has more natural pigment and needs a slightly longer processing time to lift color to lighter stages. It can tolerate heat well and yet is prone to over processing by stylists because of the slightly higher tolerance to heat.

- Will appear full-bodied
- Holds styles well
- Can tolerate higher amounts of heat
- Can be resistant to hair coloring and chemical relaxers

HAIRCOLOR SECRET

Paul Speaking: During my 17 years in the beauty business, I noticed that hair normally takes on a slight shift in texture every five to seven years for my clients, so I adjust my color formulas, products, strength of relaxer and even transition certain clients out of relaxers. This has been invaluable knowledge for me to stay ahead of the clients' needs to offset any potential problems arising!

Coloring African American Natural and Chemically Relaxed Hair

Porosity

Porosity has been a misunderstood term in our industry. The importance of understanding porosity and the pH scale is fundamental to understanding everything from performing chemical back bar services to recommending hair care products.

Porosity relates to the structural integrity of the hair to absorb moisture, while the pH scale is what we use to determine the acidity or alkalinity of a product or chemical. It's the relationship between these two realities that helps the colorist keep the proper moisture protein balance within textured hair. The pH scale guides our product choice, timing and after care products to control porosity levels from skyrocketing!

Understanding the pH Scale

Let's start with furthering our understanding of the pH scale. The scale ranges in value from 0 to 14, with 0 being the most acidic and 14 being the most alkaline:

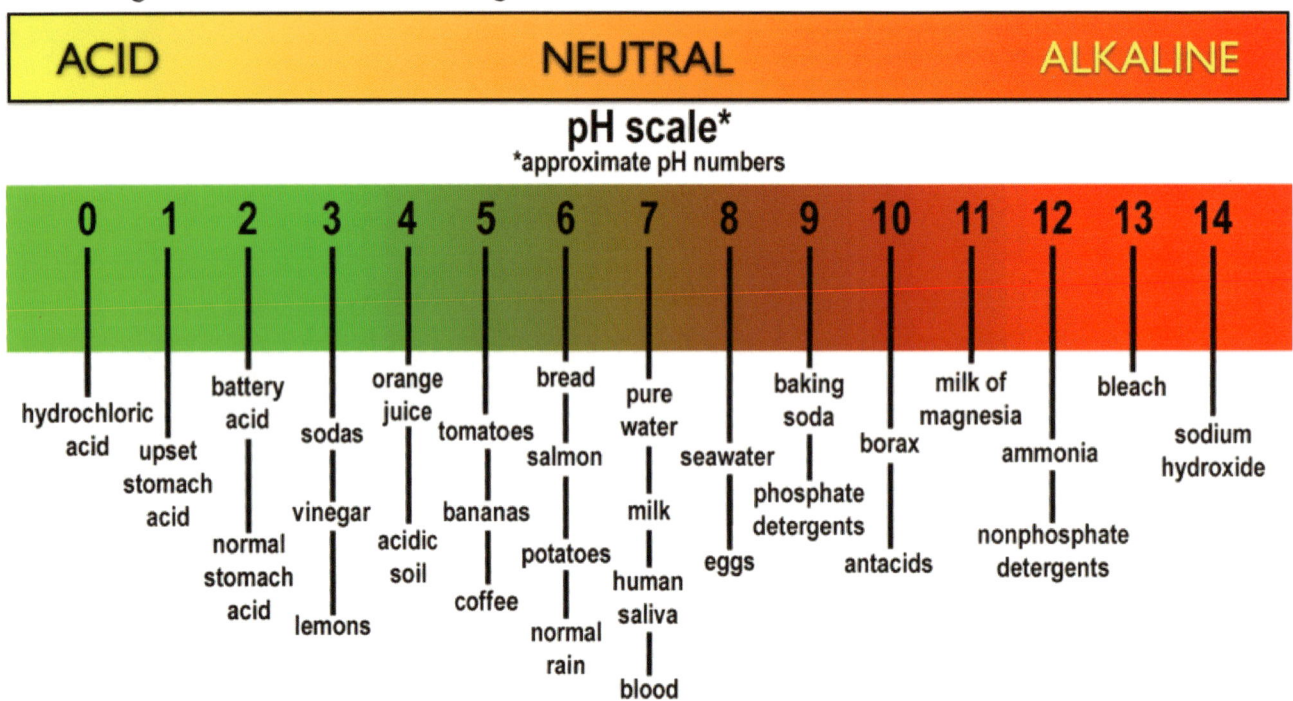

ACID — NEUTRAL — ALKALINE

pH scale*
*approximate pH numbers

pH	Example
0	hydrochloric acid
1	upset stomach acid
2	battery acid, normal stomach acid
3	sodas, lemons
4	orange juice, vinegar
5	tomatoes, acidic soil, bananas
6	bread, salmon, coffee
7	pure water, milk, potatoes, normal rain
8	seawater, human saliva, blood
9	baking soda, eggs, phosphate detergents
10	borax, antacids
11	milk of magnesia, ammonia
12	nonphosphate detergents
13	bleach
14	sodium hydroxide

Pure water carries a pH of 7 or "neutral," so anything below 7 on the scale is considered acidic and anything above 7 is considered alkali. So why is that critical to understand for curly textured hair?

The structural integrity of the hair relates to the cuticle, which is the gate to absorptions and penetration of products, chemicals and coloring products. Quite simply, when the cuticle is compact and tight, the surface of the hair strand is less porous.

Coloring African American Natural and Chemically Relaxed Hair

Compact & Tight Cuticle

The opposite occurs when the hair becomes over porous because the cuticle layer is excessively raised due to over exposure of chemicals, heating implements and sun exposure.

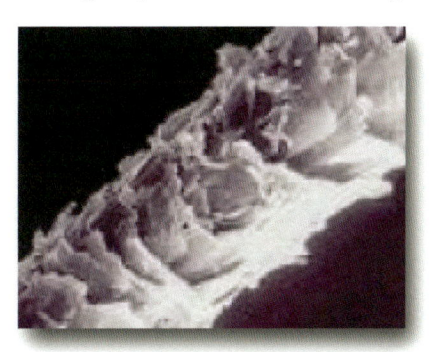

Overly Porous Hair

The cuticle is greatly affected by the pH associated with water and the products we use on the hair. Hair ranges between 4.5 and 5.5 on the pH scale, while pure water on the hair creates a more porous environment to raise the cuticle layer all by itself because water is naturally more alkaline than hair. This is where the acidic shampoos and conditioners bring the hair back into balance by closing the cuticle back down and keeping dryness and brittleness under control.

Remember, to be successful in coloring textured or relaxed hair, you have to keep the moisture **inside** the hair shaft by closing the cuticle shut. Acidic products are what closes the cuticle and keep the hair from damage, while alkaline products open the cuticle to cause change within the cortex. That's why it's imperative in choosing the right products and knowing how to use them properly makes all the difference in the health and integrity of the hair.

It is important to be knowledgeable about the pH scale which is based a "Logarithmic" scale: each change in number means a tenfold change in which two adjacent values increase or decrease by a factor of 10.

Coloring African American Natural and Chemically Relaxed Hair

For example, a pH of 3 is ten times more acidic than a pH of 4, and 100 times more acidic than a pH of 5.

- pH 3 to 4 = 10 X's more acidic
- pH 3 to 5 = 10 X 10 = 100 X's more acidic

Similarly, a pH of 9 is 10 times more alkaline than a pH of 8, and 100 more alkaline than a pH of 7.

- pH 7 to 8 = 10X's more alkaline
- pH 7 to 9 = 10 X 10 = 100 X's more alkaline

So with hair being at a pH of 5 and water at 7, you can now see how critical it is when you climb up the pH scale just a few short numbers.

That's why the colorist who understands the pH scale as it relates to porosity will be able to be aware of how to choose the appropriate coloring products(semi ,demi or permanent color) or hair care products for controlling the levels of alkalinity that come from the chemicals we use on the hair.

Logarithmic Scale

A logarithmic scale is a scale of measurement that displays the value of a physical quantity using intervals corresponding to orders of magnitude, rather than a standard linear scale.

A simple example is a chart whose vertical or horizontal axis has equally spaced increments that are labeled 1, 10, 100, 1000, instead of 1, 2, 3, 4. Each unit increase on the logarithmic scale thus represents an exponential increase in the underlying quantity for the given base (10, in this case).

Presentation of data on a logarithmic scale can be helpful when the data covers a large range of values. The use of the logarithms of the values rather than the actual values reduces a wide range to a more manageable size.

Coloring African American Natural and Chemically Relaxed Hair

Summary:

- The more you understand the basic structure of hair, the more you will know about how texture affects the hair coloring process.

- Remember the greater the diameter of the hair the coarser the texture, the less diameter, the finer the hair.

- Texture is always referred to as the feel of the hair and the category of hair you're servicing.

- The condition of the hair relates to the porosity of the hair.

- The pH value is the acidic or alkaline environment that alters the hair texture through the use of chemicals, haircare products or substance (water) .

The Theory of Haircolor Does Not Change

Texture and porosity levels will vary in great degrees depending on whether or not the hair has been chemically altered. This does not change the fact that we still have to work within the laws of haircolor.

At this point we should mention that when coloring natural and chemically relaxed African American hair, the haircolor theory does not change.

In this next section, as a refresher, we will review 10 of the most important laws of haircolor and the rules pertaining to gray coverage. Then we will discuss how to work within these rules when it comes to working on natural and chemically relaxed African-American hair.

10 Most Important Laws of Haircolor

#1

Manufacturers Make Haircolor to Work Best on:

Average Texture

and

Normal Porosity
(something we rarely work on)

Manufacturers make haircolor to work best on average texture and normal porosity, which, in my opinion, **is something on which we rarely work**.

Stop for a minute and think about how many customers you serve on the average day. Now how many of those customers have average texture and normal porosity?

Chances are very few, especially if you're working on chemically treated hair or even natural hair that is either very fine or very coarse.

So with this fact in mind, we are now going to have to alter the chemical process of haircolor in order to make it work for us. We will do this by altering the timing, strength of developers and selecting a haircolor type (for example, temporary color, demi-color, permanent hair color or bleaches) to make them perform for us in a way that they really were not designed to do.

This is not a problem, as you will see later in this book. We will give you charts that will enable you to make your haircolor formulations extremely easy to follow and understand.

In working with African-American hair types and chemically relaxed hair, the two major factors in which we need to have a thorough understanding of is the, in-depth knowledge of **texture and porosity**.

Curly textured hair that grows away from scalp will not have the ability to hold and retain natural oils and, therefore, will usually appear to be on the drier side.

Once the hair has been chemically altered by the use of chemical relaxers, it is now put into a new category and thus becomes even more porous and fragile to work with when performing a haircolor service.

Coloring African American Natural and Chemically Relaxed Hair

Herein lies the big difference between working with African-American hair and other hair types such as Caucasian hair or Asian hair.

#2
Secrets of Porosity

> **Haircolor Secret**
> *Porous hair will always Grab Ash tone and Reject Warm Tones*

Porous hair will always grab ash tones and reject warm tones.

Think about that sentence for a moment - porous hair, hair that's porous, and it doesn't matter how the porosity happened. It doesn't matter if it's been chemically altered with a relaxer, perm or hair color. It doesn't matter if she spent 2 weeks in the Florida sunshine baking her hair. It doesn't matter if she uses a flat-iron or curling iron every day. It doesn't matter care how the porosity occurred in the hair. The fact is that it is porous which means that whatever color you put on that hair, it's going to grab the ash tones and reject the warm tones.

Now, why is this important? It is important to understand because most hair color is made with what is call blended bases - meaning that they are not 100% pure in tone.

Let's take a hypothetical situation.

A client comes in to you; she's been tinted blonde. Let's say, for example, she has had a very heavy bleached highlighted look. And you decide it needs to have some color put back in and warmed up a bit, so you mix up some 8G, level 8 with a gold base, and put it on roots to ends. Thirty minutes later, what do you have? Chances are the hair will be green hair.

WHY????

At this point you may be asking yourself if it is gold hair color…. "Why is it green? I don't understand."

Well, that's because many manufacturers put green in gold colors.

Now, you may say to me, "Why do they do that? That doesn't make sense to me!"

Remember, manufacturers make haircolor to work on what?

Average Texture, Normal Porosity

Coloring African American Natural and Chemically Relaxed Hair

Average texture hair, when you lighten it, gives you what color? It gives you warmth, which is red or gold.

Now, imagine if you are already getting gold from the hair and you put on a gold tint (level 8G, with a gold base). Gold on top of gold is going to produce what - more gold – or brassiness, or what can be called "bold gold."

So, to keep us from getting bold gold hair color, manufacturers say, "Let's put some green in there to subdue that extra gold that they're going to get when they put this color on."

And that works great as long as you're using it on the intended person, as long as you're using it on somebody with darker hair. But the minute you use it on someone who has light porous hair, it's going to grab the ash, the green that's in that product. It's going to grab it, and it's going to reject the warm (gold or red). It's not going to get the warmth. It's not going to get the red. It's not going to get the gold. It's going to reject it. And when we dry the hair, it's going to be green. This is a key to understanding hair color.

#3

Secrets of Porosity

Haircolor Secret
Porosity can make a temporary color permanent and a permanent color temporary.

Understanding Temporary Haircolor

This is a really big one. Porous hair can make a temporary color permanent and a permanent haircolor temporary.

There are 4 types of haircolor.

1. Temporary haircolor
2. Semi-permanent haircolor
3. Demi haircolor
4. Permanent haircolor

Let's discuss these briefly, because there's a lot of confusion out there about this.

Coloring African American Natural and Chemically Relaxed Hair

The first one is the weakest one of all. It's called temporary haircolor. Temporary haircolor is made with what is called pre-oxidized dye molecules. In other words, you do not need a catalyst to get the color to work. The dye molecules have been pre-oxidized.

It's a large haircolor molecule. It only has the ability to adhere to the outer layer of the hair. It does not have the ability to go into the cortex layer of the hair (*as long as the cuticle of the hair is in good condition*). It sits on top of the cuticle layer of the hair, and as soon as you wash it, it washes away.

That's how temporary haircolor works, assuming you put it on – what - **average texture, normal porosity.** The minute you put it on hair that's not normal or average will it still be temporary? Not normal or average means it's not normal porosity or average texture, such as having tint or a chemical relaxer on her hair. It now becomes more permanent because the cuticle layer has been altered or lifted now allowing the temporary hair color to submerge itself between the cuticle layers and, if severe enough, even into the cortex of the hair.

Understanding Semi-permanent Haircolor

So let's look at the second type of haircolor - **semi-permanent**.

Many people think they have semi-permanent color in their salon, and they don't. They actually have a demi-color and they think (or they've been told) it's a semi-permanent color. They're very different.

A true semi-permanent color has 2 types of dye molecules, but they're both pre-oxidized, meaning you do not use any kind of a catalyst. Semi-permanent colors have large dye molecules, just like the temporary color haircolor. It also has some smaller dye molecules that are able to get between the cuticle layers. Again, it only has the ability to adhere to the outer layer of the hair, unless you put the client under a dryer or if her hair is porous.

#4

Secrets of: Demi-Colors vs Semi-Permanent Color

> A semi-permanent color is a lotion type product that is poured straight out of the bottle onto the hair. It is never mixed with anything else.
>
> If the directions call for mixing the color with any other type of substance (powders, crystals, tablets, developers or lotions of any kind), it is not a true semi-permanent color. In my book, it is a demi-permanent color.

The way you know the difference between a semi-permanent color and a demi-color is a semi-permanent color is a lotion-type product. You pour it directly out of the bottle and onto the hair. That's it. You do not mix it with anything. No liquids, no peroxide, no pills, no powders, nothing. You take it right out of the bottle and pour it on the hair.

Now, you can apply this color to the hair and put a plastic cap over it and put your client under the hairdryer for about 20 minutes. Under the hairdryer, the heat will swell the cuticle layer a little bit, and that will allow those smaller dye molecules absorb a little bit deeper into the hair shaft, but it does not have the ability to go into the cortex.

Semi- permanent haircolor is a very good color choice to use on many chemically relaxed clients (as long as they want to go darker), because there is no need for strong developers and they leave the hair in great condition.

Also, these semi-permanent colors work great as a toner over pre-lightened hair, as you will see when we get into the color formulation sections in this book.

Understanding Demi-color

Let's talk about to the third category: Demi color

Demi haircolor also has 2 types of dye molecules. It has the semi-permanent haircolor molecule that adheres to the outside layer of the hair, but it also has oxidative dye molecules that do go into the hair and slightly penetrate the cortex. It does not go in as deep as permanent haircolor, but it does have the ability to penetrate the cortex slightly.

Demi color goes into the hair, as well as on the outside of the hair. That's why when you complete a demi color service, usually the hair has intense shine because the color is not just inside the hair, it's also outside, so it coats the hair and gives it an intense shine.

All demi colors are an oxidative tint, meaning that a catalyst must be used with it. That catalyst is usually some kind of lotion. Manufacturers may call it emulsion or some funny name. But the catalyst is always going to be one of 2 things. It's either going to be some kind of derivative of ammonia, or some kind of a derivative of peroxide. It has to be. Because it's an oxidative tint, you have to have something that's going to create the oxidation process. Any time you mix 2 products together (Color and Developer), you're making an oxidative tint, which also means that your customer may get roots.

Some demi colors do have ammonia, which means that this type of demi-color may give you some lift. I have 2 demi colors in my salon: one has no ammonia and one has some ammonia. With the one that has some ammonia, I know that I can get at least one level of lift with that. The one that has no ammonia, I don't get any lift.

Demi colors are fantastic. Over the years I have actually, taken many people out of permanent color and put them into demi color.

Think about those brunettes who are turning red. They're complaining to you every time they come in saying, *"I want my hair to be a nice, rich brown, but I hate this red that I see all the time,"* the reason you're getting red is because you're lifting them too much with a permanent color.

Let's take a hypothetical situation: A lady has medium brown hair, level 4, but she's got some gray. You're using permanent color, let's say you're using level 4 because you want her color to look very natural, the same color she has. But, she comes back 4 or 5 weeks later and her hair has turned a shade of red. It's not going to be screaming red, but I'm talking like a red hue on her hair. It's because the permanent color that was used works on the oxidation process, has lightened her natural pigment in order to contributed artificial dye. When the artificial dye wears away, what's left is her natural pigment that has been lightened. So, she perceives it as being red, and it is red.

What you want to do is take her out of permanent color and use a demi color because a demi color doesn't lift as much. Some demi colors don't lift at all and some will lift slightly.

Because of the fact that demi colors are very gentle to the hair and also will give you good gray coverage makes them an ideal type of hair color to use on African-American hair types, both natural African-American hair and chemically relaxed African-American hair. These hair types will benefit greatly from the use of demi-colors.

Coloring African American Natural and Chemically Relaxed Hair

As you will see when we began our discussion on color formulations, many of the colors that you will be using will be in the demi-haircolor category.

#5

Secrets of Demi-color

Haircolor Secret
When using a progressive tint ie:(Demi- Color) always remember...
Depth, on Top of Depth, Will Always Produce More Depth!

When using a demi-color for this type of work, it is important to understand how it differs from permanent color so that you can better predict your outcome.

As you know, permanent color swells the cuticle layer of the hair, penetrates the hair shaft, gets into the cortex and lightens the natural pigmented hair and the non-pigmented, while simultaneously depositing artificial pigment into the hair. This makes all the hair (gray and pigmented) the same even color.

With a demi type color (also known as progressive tints or deposit-only tints), if a tint is used on salt and pepper colored hair that is a lighter shade than the darker natural color hair, all the hair will not be the same color at the end.

And by the same token, if a demi-color is dark or slightly darker than the client's natural color hair is used, it may come out too dark depending on the amount of gray vs. pigmented hair.

Let me explain:

Because a "deposit-only" tint can only go dark, it will darken gray (non-pigmented) hair, but keep in mind, it will also darken dark (pigmented) hair as well.

So if a demi-color (deposit-only color) is put on gray / white hair, you will get your desired depth and tone of the tint.

But if a demi-color (depth) is put on hair that is pigmented (already has its own depth), you are putting depth of color on top of depth of color (with no lift), which can only produce a deeper darker depth of color.

Coloring African American Natural and Chemically Relaxed Hair

Haircolor Secret
Always use the most <u>Gentle</u> product first and if it doesn't do the job then go to a more <u>Aggressive</u> product.

Coloring African American Natural and Chemically Relaxed Hair

#6

The Secret of when to use a Demi-color *vs.* Permanent color:

Use a *Demi- color* any time you want to:
- Stay the same level
- Go darker
- Stay the same level and change the tone.

Use a *Permanent color* any time you want to go lighter or brighter.

This is the secret of when to use a demi color versus a permanent color.

Which one should I use, when?

Use the demi color anytime you want to either stay the same level or go darker or stay the same level and change the tone.

If a client comes in, for example, and she's a level 4 with some gray in her hair or her hair lacks luster. You want to brighten it up, stay the same level, or you may want to change the tone. She's a level 4, so you might want to put a red demi color to change the tone, give her some red, and give her some vibrancy. Or, if you want to go darker, use a demi color. To go darker, you do not need permanent color 99% of the time.

Now you want to use a permanent color anytime you want to go lighter or brighter.

A different scenario – the client comes in who is a level 5. If she wants to be a 7 orangey-redhead, you've got to use permanent color. You cannot lift her from level 5 to a level 7 with demi color. The rule of thumb is, if she wants to go lighter or brighter, use permanent color. If she wants to stay the same level, go darker, or stay the same level and maybe change the tone a little bit, use your demi color.

Understanding Permanent Haircolor

I'm going to start off this discussion about permanent haircolor by telling you a little secret.

#7

Secrets of Permanent Haircolor

Haircolor Secret
Permanent haircolor isn't really permanent.

Yep, that's right. Permanent haircolor does permanently alter the structure of the hair during the oxidative process. However, the dye itself will fade a certain degree leaving the hair a very different color 5 weeks after the color service than the day of the service.

And so here then lies the problem with permanent haircolor.

Permanent haircolor (just to give a quick review) is made with 100% "Oxidative Dyes". These are dyes that change their molecular structure when mixed with a catalyst.

The most popular catalyst used in haircoloring is hydrogen peroxide (also known as developer). Although, presently, there are manufacturers promoting other types of catalysts such as "Enzymes" to try and make us think that theirs is better or different.

Their "enzymes" are nothing more than a derivative of hydrogen peroxide. (A derivative is a substance that is made from another substance but may take on another form, like ice is a derivative of water.)

When the developer comes in contact with the ammonia in permanent haircolor, it creates a gas that kick starts the oxidative process. During the oxidative process, several actions take place simultaneously:

1) The tiny color molecules begin to grow very slowly.

2) When the color is applied to the hair, the oxidative process begins to swell the cuticle layer of the hair, allowing the color molecules to penetrate into the cortex of the hair.

3) The natural color pigments in the cortex are being lightened at the same time.

Coloring African American Natural and Chemically Relaxed Hair

Once the color molecules are in the cortex of the hair, they begin to grow and grow and grow until they are so large that they cannot come back out of the same hole from which they entered.

Once the development time is complete, the hair is shampooed and the new color is present. This, of course, is an over-simplified explanation of what happens, but you get the idea.

One of the hardest things for many hairdressers to understand is how to predict what the exposed contributing color pigment will be when an oxidative tint is applied.

Until you can understand this and know how to work with it, you will never be successful in your color formulations.

This topic is discussed in great detail David's book *How Haircolor Really Works,* so it won't be rehashed it here, but what is important to know in regards to this book is how permanent haircolor works on African – American hair and chemicly relaxed hair.

We will revist this topic when we get into our haircolor Formulations section.

#8

Secrets of Permanent Haircolor

Haircolor Secret
Any time you apply an oxidative tint to the hair,
You are going to get some warmth.

Any time you apply an oxidative tint to the hair, you're going to get some warmth.

If you have a client sitting in your chair with level 1,2, 3,4 or 5 brown hair and big, brown eyes, and she says to you, **"I want my hair to be a little bit lighter brown, but I don't want to see any red, I just want a sandy brown".** Do not attempt it, because it doesn't work. You cannot go from dark brown to light brown without pulling red. It's against the law of color. She's always going to pull red. It's the story of decolorization of natural pigment. (See next page)

I know, time and time again, clients will sit in your chair and say something like that, and for some reason, we think like, *"Hum… it's never worked before, but maybe it will work this time."* And you go ahead and do it anyway, and you end up having red hair, and she ends up being very disappointed.

Coloring African American Natural and Chemically Relaxed Hair

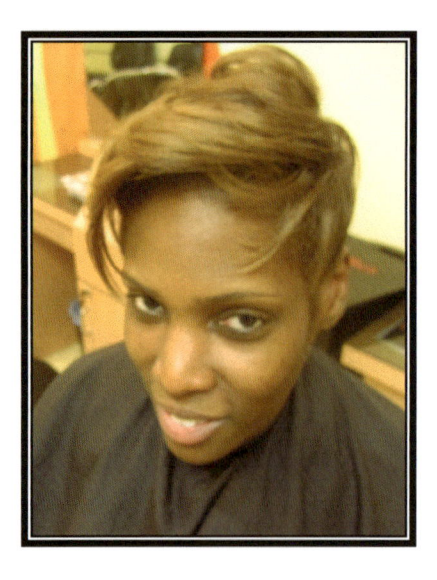

The Overall Concept of Decolorization: If you remember from your beauty school days, as you lighten out hair, it goes through what is called the **"Stages of Lift"**. It goes something like this…

Brown→Reddish Brown→Red→Orange→ Gold→Yellow→Pale Yellow

Brown to Blonde

Keep in mind; darker natural levels (levels 1-4) as in African American hair will have a strong red-orange exposed contributing pigment, when a tint is applied.

It is for this reason that I really prefer to use a demi type color, whenever possible.
It will create less warmth (because demi's produce "no lift" or "less lift") than a permanent color in the same level.

This red-orange contributing pigment makes it almost impossible to create a cool natural looking brunette unless you go very dark (which may not look very natural) or unless of course you **pre-lighten** the hair first with bleach, remove the red-orange and then tone the hair with a cool base color.

So, always keep in mind that you're in the business of controlling unwanted warm tones. That's your business. And the better you can control unwanted warm tones, the more success you're going to have in your hair colors.

#9

Secrets of Permanent Haircolor

> **Haircolor Secret**
>
> *Less Lift = Less Warmth*

Less lift equals less warmth. If you're having a problem with too much warmth, don't lift the hair so much.

The only time you want more warmth is when you want to create a redhead.

When creating a redhead, you want (and need) that red-orange contributing color pigment.

#10

Secrets of Permanent Haircolor

> *With permanent haircolor, it's the combination of:*
>
> *Tint + Exposed Contributing Color Pigment = End Color Result*

With permanent hair color, it's a combination of the tint plus the exposed contributing pigment, that equals good hair color results.

This is something that's very hard for a lot of people to understand.

If you're a painter and you're painting on a palette in order to paint a picture, you get your palette in your arm and you mix 2 colors together. For example, let's say you mixed blue and yellow and you're making green. Right?

Coloring African American Natural and Chemically Relaxed Hair

When you put that green paint on a white canvas, what color do you get? You've got a white canvas. You're an artist, a painter. Forget about hair for now. I'm talking about painting a picture. You get green and you put it on a white canvas, what color do you get? You get green.

With hair color, it doesn't work that way, because our canvas is alive. Our canvas gives us something in return. Even white hair gives something in return (yellow). So, you must realize that you need the combination of the tint. Then you've got to be able to predict what that hair's going to give you (the contributing color pigment you will get when you lift the hair) when you apply that tint on the hair, and that's going to be based on the level of your tint.

If you use a level of tint close to the natural level of your client's hair, you're not going to get much change. For example if a client has a natural level 4 and you're using a level 8 tint, you are using a dramatically different level. Therefore, you've got to realize what that level 8 tint is going to produce when applied to the level 4 head of hair. What is it going to give you back, so that it will work in combination with your tint to equal a nice hair color when she leaves the door?

This is a major key to understanding how to do great haircolor. This topic is beyond the scope of this book, but if you want more information about it you will find a very detailed explanation in David's first book, *How Haircolor Really Works*.

Haircolor Secret

Good haircolor happens when you are able to predict just how warm the natural haircolor will be and successfully use that warm color as part of your overall color formula and learn to work with it instead of trying to disguise it, pretending that it isn't there.

For more information on How Haircolor Really Works, read Volume-2 in the Haircolor Trade Secrets series titled: ***How Haircolor Really Work***

Coloring African American Natural and Chemically Relaxed Hair

Gray Coverage Rules Do Not Change

Gray Coverage Overview

Understanding gray coverage is important because it comprises the bulk of our salon clients and services in our industry and most salons.

First of all, there's no such thing as real gray hair. There is only pigmented hair (brown, red & blonde) and non-pigmented hair (white). What we perceive as being "gray hair" is actually a combination of pigmented hair mixed with white hair. The less white a person has, the grayer she tends to look. The more white a person has, the less gray she tends to look, but the more white her hair looks.

This phenomenon is best explained with something called the "Gray Scale". This is a tool used in black & white photography & film, which allows our eyes to actually see different tones of color, which are only made up of the colors black and white intermixed into verging degrees. Back in the days of black & white TV, we all knew that Lucille Ball had bright red hair even though no one had a color television. ☺

"GRAY SCALE"

It's the combination of the two strands that creates a gray appearance. This is key in understanding how to formulate for gray hair because the percentage of salt (white) pepper (pigment) will help you make the predetermined calculation before you create your formula.

To get great gray coverage, formulas should be warm because they cover better than cool formulas. When using warmth in your hair coloring we are replacing the missing underlying warmth of the non-pigmented hair.

To cover gray on natural African American hair, the formula must be aggressive enough to soften the cuticle layer for deeper penetration (20-vol) but not higher than 25-vol developer which should only be used on more dense, coarse hair. When covering gray on coarse, **relaxed hair,** 20-vol or lower is recommended because the porosity level is usually **higher for relaxed hair than natural hair.**

Coloring African American Natural and Chemically Relaxed Hair

Proper Coverage

The key to gray coverage is to select the right developer and formula for gray that is capable of softening the cuticle for deposit and less lift.

Natural texture compared to relaxed hair can be wiry and coarse with a compact cuticle. A weaker developer won't penetrate enough through the cuticle for great coverage. You will have to get past the resistant cuticle layer with a higher volume up to 25-vol . It is imperative to avoid higher developers above 25 vol. because you will get less deposit and higher lift which will blend the gray but not cover it.

Maximum deposit and the correct formulation is the goal for all gray coverage regardless of the percentages of gray.

For example:

When creating a formula for gray coverage, the constant complaint is "the color didn't cover the gray". You are right because the color formulated and applied was lighter than you expected. Any time your add 1/2 oz tone to your neutral color you automatically lighten the neutral color to a lighter level. For example: When pouring added milk in your glass of dark chocolate milk your mixture becomes lighter. This same principle happens when you mix an added tone to your(formula) neutral , the neutral is diluted by the tone, when you add ½ ounce or more in your formulation.

Note: When using a "Neutral" base color and you are adding a ½ oz tone to your formula such as gold . Always go down a level with your neutral color to avoid diluting your base color. This will give you better coverage and longer lasting wearablity for your gray hair clients.

Proper timing is another important aspect in giving your client a maximum deposit. 30- 35 minutes is usually sufficient on virgin or regrowth application. Depending on texture and density 5 extra minutes might be needed to be added on for virgin dense coarse texture.   For the mid-shaft to the ends use demi color with 10-vol developer timing will vary 5-15minutes depending upon porosity and fading.

Tradition in our industry says gray hair is more resistant than pigmented hair. This is not necessarily so. Resistance is not based on the color of the hair but rather the texture (diameter) of the hair. Dense, coarse, natural hair that is gray is much more resistant than fine or normal hair.

The remedy is to adjust your formula (1-1/2parts of color and 1 part developer),
 Slightly raise your volume of peroxide to using 25-vol developer and use finer sections applying slightly more product for better saturation. Note: This formula is to be used for dense, coarse natural texture for better penetration and deposit for gray coverage.

For more information on achieving great gray coverage, read Volume-2 in this series;
Great Gray Coverage.

Coloring African American Natural and Chemically Relaxed Hair

---

Haircolor Secret

Don't be stingy with applying color to gray hair. Apply a sufficient amount but don't over saturate to the point the color begins to drip all over the client's face.

Ash colors used alone do not cover gray as well as color formulations containing warmth. Formulations containing red or gold tones deliver the best coverage and most natural looking results. Maximum timing is the goal in getting maximum deposit and coverage. It is correctly evaluating the percentage of gray hair that will make the difference in your formulation.

---

6 - Gray Coverage Rules

In working with African-American natural and/or chemically relaxed hair, we have to realize that the rules pertaining to gray coverage do not change. Here six ground rules called:

"The 6 Secret Ground Rules of Working on Gray Hair"

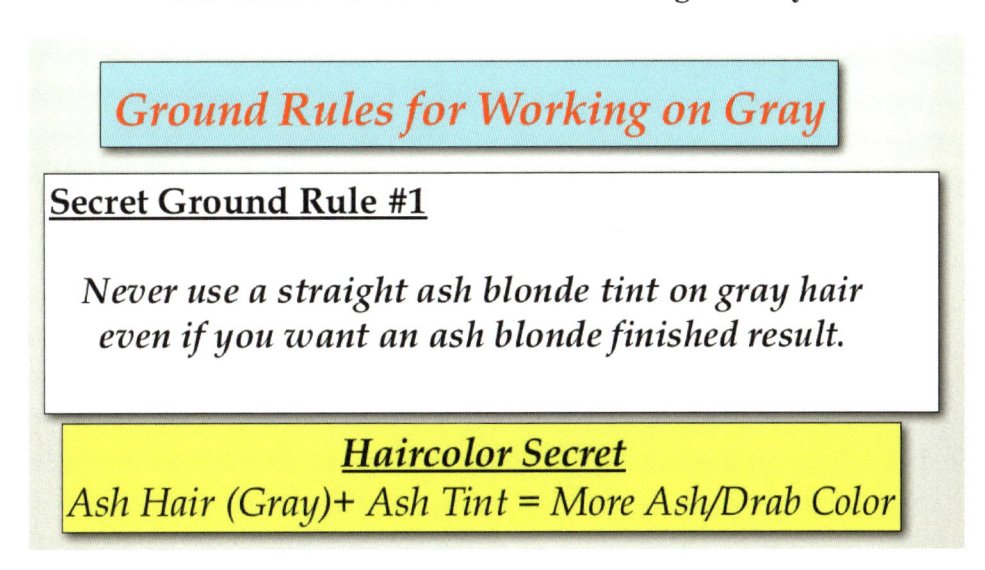

Ground Rules for Working on Gray

Secret Ground Rule #1

Never use a straight ash blonde tint on gray hair even if you want an ash blonde finished result.

Haircolor Secret
Ash Hair (Gray) + Ash Tint = More Ash/Drab Color

Ground rule #1: Never use a straight ash-blonde tint on gray hair, even if you want an ash-blonde finished result.

In the bottom yellow section, you see the hair color trade secret about ash hair. Gray hair (which is completely ash in color) plus ash tint will give you a very ash, drab color because: **ASH ON TOP OF ASH CAN ONLY GIVE YOU MORE ASH!**

Of course, every woman who comes to you with gray hair will tell you, "I want to be an ash-blonde." They all want to be ash-blondes, for some reason. So, what do we do? We cannot use ash on her hair, because she's just going to be too ash.

Coloring African American Natural and Chemically Relaxed Hair

The recommendation is to use your neutral-based colors, your N's, your N-based colors, and maybe you can use a little bit of ash or even a little bit of gold. You can warm it up with a little gold.

Your N-based colors, used alone, are a little flat-looking but when you mix them with a little gold or ash tint, they will look fine.

One more thing, the letter "N" on your swatch chart represents either "natural" or "neutral." depending on which manufacturer you use. They're interchangeable.

Ground Rules for Working on Gray

Secret Ground Rule #2

To get total gray coverage on resistant gray hair, you will need to use a level 8 blonde or darker.

(If the hair is a fine texture, level 9 may work)

Secret ground rule #2: To get total gray coverage on resistant gray hair, you need to use a level 8 blonde or darker.

The bottom line says, "If the hair is a fine texture, a level 9 may work." If you're doing color on someone who has resistant gray hair – and we're talking about blondes here, and you're not getting adequate color results, you're not covering the gray well enough. Look and see what your formula is. If your formula is like a 9N or 9A or 9G, you may have to drop that to level 8.

Now, if you think a level 8 may be too dark, what you may want to do is mix an 8 and a 9, and slowly move a little bit deeper. But most hair color manufacturers will tell you, "Don't use anything lighter than a level 8 to get guaranteed gray coverage results."

NOTE: If the hair's a FINE texture a level 9 tint may work. Why is that? Because fine-textured hair will always react faster to any chemical process than coarse-textured hair.

Remember, the coarser the hair, the more resistance it is going to be to any chemical process. And that's true if you're coloring the hair, if you're perming or relaxing the hair. Finer-textured hair will always react much quicker and much more extreme than coarse textured hair.

Coloring African American Natural and Chemically Relaxed Hair

Ground Rules for Working on Gray

Secret Ground Rule #3

Never put a straight cool red tint on gray hair.

Secret ground rule #3: Never put a straight red tint on gray hair.

You cannot just put straight red on top of white hair and expect to get good gray coverage. You need to mix it with some brown base tint. If you don't it will be pink or some real funky color.

Gray hair does not have any warmth. Warmth, we know, is gold or red. Gray hair is totally absent of all warmth.

If you PUT a straight red tint on white hair, without adding anything else to it (gold or Neutral/Natural), you're going to get the full impact of the red on top of hair that can't support it because there's not enough warmth to balance it out.

So, depending on what shade red you use, the hair can look pink, it can look mauve, it can take on some other weird funky color or it can just be incredibly bright, like "hot roots."

What you need to do is add some brown tint (gold or Neutral/Natural) into your formula.

Ground Rules for Working on Gray

The Secret Ground Rule #4

Gray hair will always turn yellow when lightened because of the pheomelanin (red-yellow) pigment which is still in the hair.

Ground rule #4: Gray/white hair will always turn yellow when lightened, because of the pheomelanin pigment that's still in the hair.

Coloring African American Natural and Chemically Relaxed Hair

I'm sure that we all have seen a person with gray/white hair and that has a yellow cast

That's because of the pheomelanin pigment that is still in the hair.

If someone with white hair spends time out in the sun and the sun has opportunity to bleach out the hair some, what you'll see a strong yellow pigmentation coming through.

So it is important to realize that when you are working over white hair in your lighter shades, you are prepared to handle this yellow tone.

Ground Rules for Working on Gray

Secret Ground Rule #5

All gray (non-pigmented) hair is not created equal and, therefore, will not react the same to tinting, bleaching or toning.

Ground rule #5: All gray hair is not created equal – therefore, it will not react the same to tinting, bleaching or toning.

Coarse textured gray (non-pigmented) hair will always react slower and be more stubborn when tinting, bleaching, toning or relaxing. Finer textured gray (non-pigmented) hair will always react quicker to tinting, bleaching, toning or relaxing.

Keep in mind that on the same head of hair, you will have a mixture of fine, medium and coarse gray (non-pigmented) hair. And in some cases, you may have to treat these different parts of the head with separate hair color formulas.

Coloring African American Natural and Chemically Relaxed Hair

Ground Rules for Working on Gray

> **Secret Ground Rule #6**
>
> *In most cases, when covering 75% to 100% gray (non-pigmented) hair, you will have to mix the desired shade with either a gold base tint or a neutral/natural base tint in order to make up for the lack of warmth in the hair.*

Ground rule #6: In most cases with 75% to 100% gray hair, you have to mix the desired shade with a gold-based tint or a neutral/natural to make up for the lack of warmth.

Now, that was already said about redheads. But in truth, it's also the same with brunettes.

Most tints are made to be put on pigmented hair, which will give a contributing color pigment of red or gold. Therefore, if working on 100% gray (non-pigmented) hair, you will have to mix in the missing tone (gold/red), or both, in order to make up for the lack of this warmth in the gray (non-pigmented) hair.

> For more information on working with gray hair, read Volume-3 in the Haircolor Trade Secrets series titled: *Great Gray Coverage*

So, What Does Change?

So far we've learned that certain things about coloring African-American hair do not change. The theory of color does not change, and the rules for working on gray-hair do not change.

So what does change?

What makes coloring African-American hair so different than coloring other hair types such as Caucasian or Asian hair?

In the next section of this book we introduce you to what we call the:

Coloring African American Natural and Chemically Relaxed Hair

The 5 Variables of Coloring African-American Hair

They are as follow:

1. The Hair's Natural Color
2. 2 Kinds of Texture
3. 3 Types of Natural Texture
4. 5 Stages of Porosity
5. 3 Types of Relaxers

Understanding the 5-Variables

A thorough understanding of the following 5 variables is necessary before we can begin to logically formulate for these various hair types and conditions.

The only constant variable in this whole formulation concept is that 99% of the time when coloring natural African-American hair you will be working on
Brown hair, levels 2,3 or 4.

Therefore, all of the haircolor formulation presented throughout the rest of this book will be **based on one constant variable**, your client sitting in the chair is going to be African-American and she will most likely be a brunette from levels 2 through 4.

We do recognize, of course, that there will be a small percentage of African-American clients who have either red hair or even blonde hair. When confronted with that scenario you would need to adjust your formulas to reflect the change in underlying pigment that we will recommend.

Coloring African American Natural and Chemically Relaxed Hair

Variable #1

THE HAIR'S NATURAL COLOR

Most African-Americans have medium to dark brown natural hair color. This is the only constant that we have in the equation

The Only Constant is Natural Color

Aside from gray hair, most African-Americans have medium to dark brown natural hair color. So this will be the starting point for most of our formulations concerning African American clients.

Melanin is pigment located inside the hair structure and gives hair its natural color. How light or dark hair is naturally and its characteristics depends on how much and what kind of melanin it contains and how that melanin is arranged in the hair.

The higher the concentration of eumelanin, the darker the hair and the larger the granules which contains the melanin. Eumelanin, which has an oval or elliptical shape is found in black and brown hair.

From a colorist point of view, the most important thing to know about melanin is what happens to it when we apply haircolor.

Lightening of Melanin:

Recognizing what depth the natural haircolor is (the Level) and what it will change into once it is lifted with the developer and the tint is deposited, allows the colorist to anticipate with confidence the final color result. How we achieve that is first understanding the equation of:

Natural color + Contributing pigment + Artificial pigment = Final color result.

Most African Americans who have large amount of eumelanin in the hair usually have problems in avoiding brassy orangey tones when lightening hair. Their darker brown hair has to overcome a tenacious amount of warm red and orange stages compared to clients of with lighter natural haircolor.

This exposure to more warmth should direct the colorist servicing African Americans clients to select haircolor or toners, that counteract any brassiness. Remember natural base level + the desired target level will help you to anticipate what amount of exposed pigment you need to use in your formula to achieved the desired tonal result.

Coloring African American Natural and Chemically Relaxed Hair

Importance of contributing pigment:

Contributing pigments are a created when the lifting or lightening process takes place on every natural hair level. When lifting and depositing, as in when lightening dark hair, warmth is exposed during stages of lightening, the hair will go through different stages of lightness and be exposed to different underlying pigments compared to light brown hair clients.

By identifying the natural level, we can determine how light the client can be lightened in a single process. Then we can anticipate (which will account for 50% of our formula) what formula to use in counteracting strong brassy undertones when lifting 3 levels or higher.

Note : When coloring dark pigment we need a greater penetration to lift more dark pigment. **So we need a stronger developer for natural hair compared to relaxed hair,** and an ash based formula to subdue the underlying warmth that is associated with dark coarse dense hair.

Rule of thumb: Dark hair will always generate strong warm tones when lifting to blond, so a toner must be used after lightening to the appropriate level in order to create natural looking color.

Haircolor Secrets

Contributing color pigment will consist of 50% of your formula. By determining the client's natural level, you will have an indication of what underlying pigment you will be creating. Then you will decide to enhance, cover or expose the contributing pigment.

Permanent color is limited in how light you can lighten in a single process color without causing too much brassiness. **Relaxed hair** will only need 20-vol developer compared to a higher volume for natural hair.

Because relaxed hair is more porous than natural hair, it takes a weaker peroxide to generate lift. Dark hair always has challenges in overcoming red and orange stages of contributing pigment in reaching lighter levels without brassiness.
Cool or ash formulas are best utilized to counteract unnecessary warm tones.

The Contributing Color Pigment Chart

The Contributing Color Pigment Chart on the next page will show you exactly what happens as you lighten someone's natural haircolor.

In the center of the chart is the *"Level"* of the hair, on the left is the *"Color Swatch"* of that Level and on the right is the *"Contributing Color"* that will appear as you lift the natural haircolor.

Coloring African American Natural and Chemically Relaxed Hair

NOTE: Contributing color pigment is also known as: **Underlying Color Pigment, Exposed Contributing Color, Residual Color Value** and a few other names.
They all have the same meaning.

NATURAL HAIRCOLOR	LEVEL	CONTRIBUTING COLOR PIGMENT	
LIGHTEST BLONDE	10	PALE YELLOW	*LEVELS – 6 to 10*
VERY LIGHT BLONDE	9	YELLOW	
LIGHT BLONDE	8	DARK YELLOW	
MEDIUM BLONDE	7	GOLD	
DARK BLONDE	6	GOLD ORANGE	
LIGHT BROWN	5	ORANGE	*LEVELS – 1 to 5*
MEDIUM BROWN	4	RED ORANGE	
DARK BROWN	3	DARK RED ORANGE	
VERY DARK	2	RED BROWN	
BLACK	1	DARK RED BROWN	

Copyright © 2007-2014 by David Velasco: All Rights Reserved : www.Haircolortradesecrets.com

Coloring African American Natural and Chemically Relaxed Hair

Variable #2

2 KINDS OF TEXTURE

Defining the word TEXTURE

We discussed earlier in this book on page 15 that African American texture that there are two different meanings.

For the purpose of writing this book and for understanding our formulation concepts and charts, we will be defining in depth the meaning of both types of texture intermittently.

In this section of our study of African American hair we will concentrate on three common textures that are most common in the African American or Multi-ethnic Cultural.

- **Wavy Texture**
- **Curly Texture**
- **Kinky Texture**

Two Kinds of Hair Texture

1. The Diameter of Each Hair Strand
2. The Natural Curl Formation OR Texture:

3 Types of Hair (Diameter) TEXTURE:

1. Fine
2. Medium
3. Coarse

Coloring African American Natural and Chemically Relaxed Hair

The Diameter of A Hair Strand

Secrets of Texture

Secrets of Texture

Think of Hair Texture as Fabric

COARSE — Coarse Texture Hair is like Denim

AVERAGE — Average Texture Hair is like Cotton

FINE — Fine Texture Hair is Like Silk

Coarse Hair   **Fine Hair**

Think of hair texture (as in the diameter of the hair) as a fabric. Think of coarse hair, which is the top one and thickest of all, as denim. Think of average texture as cotton and fine texture as silk.

Thinking of hair as fabric allows us to understand that finer texture hair cannot take as much abuse as average or coarse texture hair. You cannot bleach it the same way; you cannot tint it the same way; you cannot relax it the same way. It's very, very different.

Coloring African American Natural and Chemically Relaxed Hair

Let me future explain the fabric analogy.

When I (David) was a kid in junior high school, my mother bought me a brand new pair of blue jeans. (We used to call them dungarees back in those days.) They were stiff as a board. The first thing she would have to do is wash them about 25 or 30 times in the washing machine before I could wear them to school. The more you washed jeans, the better they got. After a couple hundred washings, they really got nice and comfortable. (These were the days before "Pre-washed" jeans came on the market)

Try doing that with a silk blouse. How many washings in a washing machine can a silk blouse take - none. One or 2 and it will be destroyed.

Think of hair the same way. If the hair is a fine texture, you have to use the most gentle product you can to make it work. Instead of using a permanent color, use a demi color. Instead of using a strong relaxer, use a milder relaxer.

Your goal should always be, in every haircolor or relaxer service, to use the gentlest product first to do the job. If that doesn't work, then you can move to a more aggressive product.

3 Types of Curl Diameter Texture:

1- Fine:

- Very easy to process yet is susceptible to being over processed because of its diameter
- **Does not have the same structure and amount of protein as coarse hair**
- Appears limp and flyaway not holding a curl or style
- The coloring penetration is faster so the use of lower volume of coloring and lightening services is recommended.

2- Medium or Average:

- Indicates a middle-range of the size of the hair shaft
- Considered normal and poses no special considerations regarding processing and chemical services
- Normal amount of keratin protein
- Normal processing time for coloring

3- Coarse:

- Strongest but usually the hardest to process
- Can be resistant to hair-coloring
- Takes longer for coloring process to infuse pigment into the cortex because it has more pigment than the other two textures.

Coloring African American Natural and Chemically Relaxed Hair

Variable #3

3 TYPES OF NATURAL TEXTURE

Introduction to the 3 Types of Curl Formation, also known as Texture:

Hair texture (formation) varies in individuals and ethnicity. And each texture has its own size measurement in separate areas of the same head. For example, a client may have fine hair at the crown of the head but coarse hair around the occipital bone.

The term *"Texture"* is used today to describe what hair type a person has, such as wavy, curly or kinky curl pattern. The various combinations of these hair types can be found in every ethnic background.

In today's hair fashion, ***using tools such as rollers, crimp irons and curling wands can create texture***. The look of texture can be worn naturally (wash & wear) or enhanced with twists, locks or dreads.

Whatever the style a client has, the defining nature of texture is measured by the degree of fineness to coarseness of hair that varies according to each individual.

The degree of fineness to coarseness will make up the character of that hair texture.

African Americans who have intertwined with different racial backgrounds have genetically produced a large variety of curl patterns from wavy to kinky. This takes into consideration special handling and care regarding hair care products and chemical processes.

The Natural Curl Formation OR Texture

3 Types of Natural Curl Formation OR Texture:

1. **Wavy**
2. **Curly**
3. **Kinky**

Wavy | Curly | Kinky

Coloring African American Natural and Chemically Relaxed Hair

Wavy

1. **Wavy Texture**

- TEXTURE:
    - From a loose wave to a deeper, tighter wave
- DENSITY:
    - Fine to coarse
- ELASTICITY:
    - Good return on stretching
    - Fine to medium
- POROSITY:
    - Stage 2 without chemical, Stage 3 with chemical
    - Coarser wavy hair with a slightly raised cuticle
    - May have a problem with frizz

The wavy texture has resiliency but, the natural sebum (oil) tends not to be able to fully wrap around the hair shaft. It's the exact opposite for finer wavier hair, which gets more oil running down the hair shaft. It is more compatible with coloring or lightening.

Coloring African American Natural and Chemically Relaxed Hair

Curly

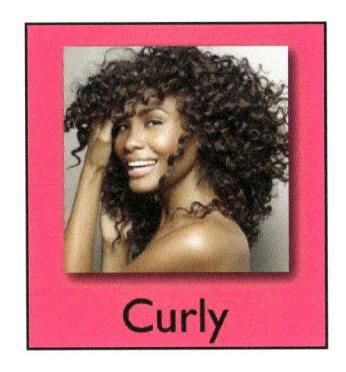

2. **Curly Texture**

- TEXTURE:
    - From corkscrew and ringlets to shaped curls forming into coils
    - Can lean more on the frizzy textured side
- DENSITY:
    - Combination of different densities within the hair
    - Has volume with less movement because of the tightness of the curl
- ELASTICITY:
    - Good return is minimal when stretched
- POROSITY:
    - Stage 2 without chemical, Stage 3 with chemical raised cuticle
    - Constantly tangles and frizzes

This texture constantly loses moisture because of the raised cuticle becoming frizzy with dry ends. Products that are hydrating and frequent steam treatments are necessary when applying permanent hair coloring or chemical texturizers to loosen the curl pattern.

Coloring African American Natural and Chemically Relaxed Hair

Kinky

3. Kinky Texture

- TEXTURE:
    - Consists of three curl patterns: Coily, Very Coily and Tight Coils
- DENSITY:
    - Compact
- ELASTICITY:
    - Minimal return when stretched
    - Lacks elasticity
- POROSITY:
    - Stage 2 without chemical, Stage 3 with chemical
    - Raised cuticle
    - Constantly knots and tangles

Kinky hair can feel cottony, spongy and crunchy when you touch it. This hair texture is coarse but very fragile and prone to breakage. It also lacks moisture because of the curl pattern raises the cuticle. Hair care is very important when servicing kinky hair.

Coloring African American Natural and Chemically Relaxed Hair

A Few Words About Density

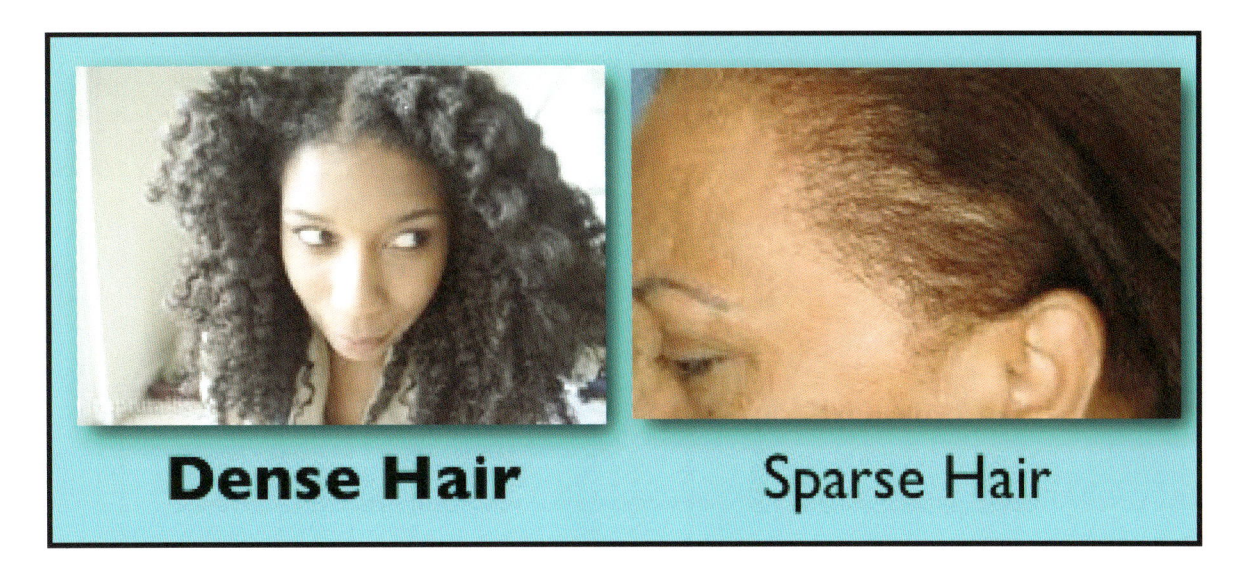

Dense Hair **Sparse Hair**

Density tells us how thick or thin the client's hair is. Density in its pure definition is the amount of "hair strands per square inch" on the head. The key word is "amount". We've all heard people described as having "thick" hair. This expression means that the combination of density and texture has produced a thick head of hair.

While density relates to how much "hair volume" per square inch is on the head, texture relates the diameter of each strand, with coarse being the thickest. So often stylists overlook the fact that a client's texture can be coarse but fine in density, or thick in density but fine in texture.

Good color happens when a colorist knows how dense the texture is on which he/she is working with, this helps the colorist to begin selecting the appropriate product to use and how much of this product is needed to adequately change the tone of the hair without weakening the cortex, which is it the core strength of the hair.

Note: Curlier and Kinky textures that are dense will diffuse light reflection from the color on the hair shaft. The recommendation is to add a little more lift, which will give you more warmth, by adding (lighting crème) to your formula without adding more developer. This will increase your light reflection on the hair strand without further damaging the hair shaft.

A good colorist is always aware of the damage created by using excessive high volume developer and utilizes only what is needed based on density and texture.

It's not uncommon to have various textures and densities throughout the head; for example, the hair may be dense and coarse around the occipital area of the head but finer in the crown section and frontal portion of the head.

The larger the hair follicle, the thicker the strand will be. The smaller the diameter of hair strand the finer the texture. Our formula will simply have to provide for deeper penetration because of the width of

Coloring African American Natural and Chemically Relaxed Hair

the fine hair texture is dictating that we use higher ammonia lift without using a higher developer but still control the level of porosity to avoid damage to the fine texture and avoid color fading.

This is why there is no need to subcategorized hair texture, when it comes to identifying curl formation. Because each hair property is independent of one another it helps the colorist in selecting which color product to use, and how intense the developer needs to be when lifting or depositing haircolor into the hair. The hair properties are:

- Texture
- Density
- Porosity
- Elasticity

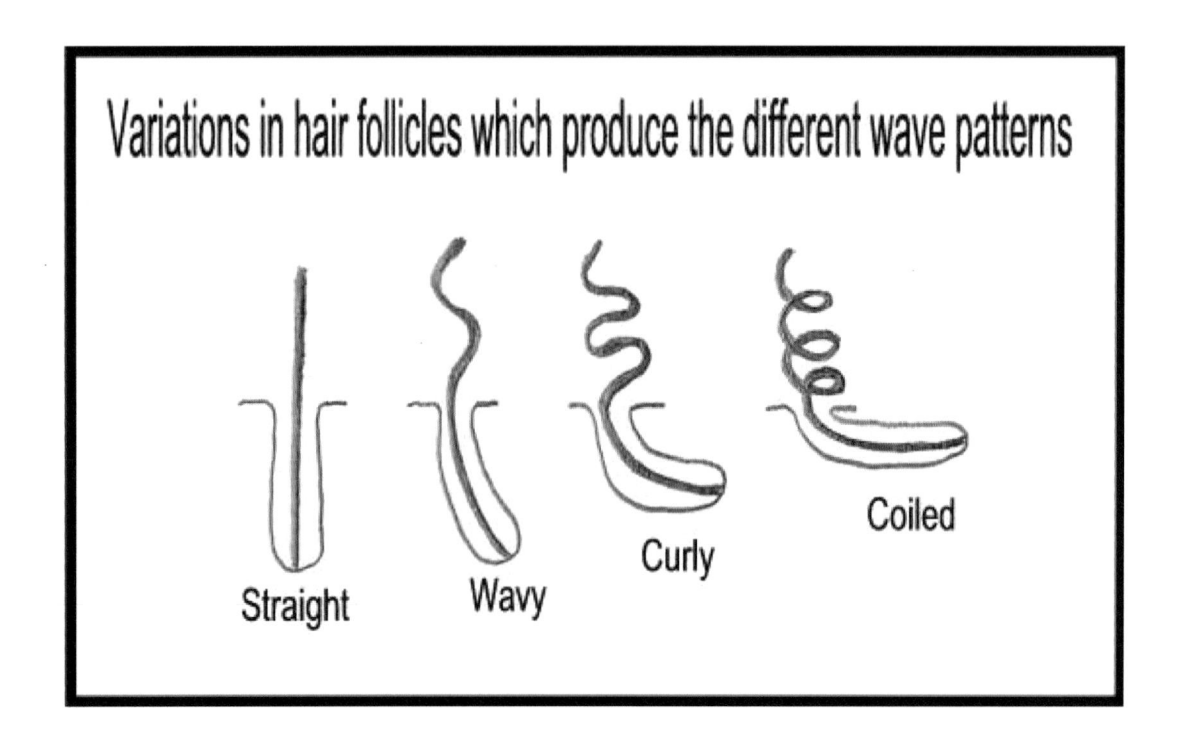

Variations in hair follicles which produce the different wave patterns

Straight — Wavy — Curly — Coiled

Coloring African American Natural and Chemically Relaxed Hair

These photos show you a cross-sectional view of the three major ethnic groups

African Hair

African-American Hair is "Elliptical" in shape to the point of almost flat in some areas. This Shape is what makes it curly or frizzy

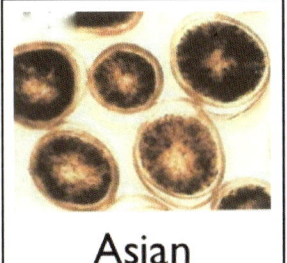

Asian Hair

Asian hair is the most Cylindrical in shape, almost "TUBULAR". This is why it is so Straight

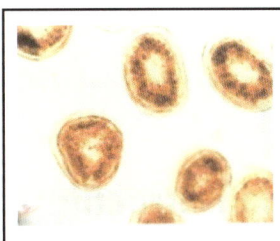

Caucasian Hair

Caucasian hair is a mix of "Cylindrical" and "Bean" Shape strands which can very from straight, wavy or curly

Variable #4

5 STAGES OF POROSITY

5 Stages of Porosity

The next variable that we have to understand is a thorough comprehension of porosity. For the purposes of this book and in trying to standardize a system of teaching haircolor formulation for African-American hair, it is crucial that we breakdown porosity into five different categories or what we call the **Stages of Porosity. Th**ey are as follow:

5 Stages of Porosity

Stage 1: Chemical free textured hair with compact, tight cuticle

Stage 2: Natural texture or mild chemicals with slightly raised cuticle

Stage 3: Exposure to chemicals both relaxers and permanent color

Stage 4: Over exposure to high alkaline chemicals

Stage 5: Breakage, over exposure to chemical products

The Five Stages of Porosity

Porosity is the ability of the hair to retain and absorb moisture such as water, hair products and chemicals within the cuticle layer of the hair and penetrating in the cortex.

Porosity is dictated by the texture of the hair, the integrity of the hair, the products used on the hair and the hair's exposure to heat (mechanical, chemical or environmental).

Resistant hair, which has a compact cuticle layer, may need longer processing time and a stronger developer, when compared to overly porous hair whose cuticle is highly raised causing the hair to be constantly dry and rough. This type of hair may need a semi – permanent color to help reduce the porosity by depositing only without the use of a developer.

There can be various degrees of porosity on a single strand of hair. For example, the new re-growth at the scalp can be resistant, while the mid-shaft may be normal and the ends of the hair overly porous. This means that the colorist will need to adjust his/her formula accordingly for the different stages of porosity or the end result will be uneven.

Coloring African American Natural and Chemically Relaxed Hair

---

Haircolor Secret

A good indicator in knowing what level of porosity you are working with is to visually notice the difference from scalp to the ends.
The greater contrast from scalp to ends, the greater the porosity.

This will help guide you in knowing the condition of the hair so you can adjust your product selection and formulation based on the type of texture you are coloring.

No matter what degree of porosity, your formulation will always be a reflection of the condition of the hair.

Keep in mind with healthy hair you formulate to counteract warm undertones, with damaged hair your formulate against hair going too drab.

The Five Stages of Porosity are:

1. Resistant
2. Slightly Porous
3. Normal Porosity
4. Overly Porous
5. Excessively Porous Hair

Each one of these Stages represents how much the cuticle layer has been lifted up from the hair strand. The higher the cuticle is lifted the more porous the hair will become causing potential damage to the cortex.

Compare this to normal porosity, which allows moisture to pass through to the cortex of the hair and at the same time, maintains moisture so the hair is sufficiently sealed against external moisture and humidity.

When the hair is excessively porous, the cuticle layer is either damaged, lifted up or completely missing leaving the hair vulnerable to shedding, constant split ends and prone to breakage.

The following are descriptions of the 5 stages of porosity, which we will use in our haircolor formulations later in this book.

Coloring African American Natural and Chemically Relaxed Hair

Stage 1: --- Resistant

- Chemical free texture
- Compact tight cuticle layer
- Minimal use of hot tools
- Normal environmental exposure
- Water doesn't penetrate the hair shaft easily before shampooing
- May require a slightly longer processing time when permanent color is applied

Stage 2: -- Slightly Porous

- Natural texture or mild chemicals
- Limited use of hot tools
- Slightly raised cuticle
- Some sun exposure or chlorine water
- Takes a while for water to penetrate hair shaft before shampoo
- Doesn't easily tangle
- Requires a slightly longer processing time when permanent color is applied

Stage 3: -- Normal Porosity

- Exposure to chemicals, either relaxers and/or permanent color
- Moderately raised cuticle
- Regular usage of heating implements
- When combing, the hair doesn't tangle easily
- Normal elasticity
- Processes color in an average amount of time

Stage 4: -- Overly Porous

- Over exposure to high alkaline chemicals
- Dull and frizzy because of a swollen cuticle
- Constant use of heating implements
- Easily tangles into knots when combing dry or wet
- Excessive amount of exposure to sun, wind and cold weather
- Elasticity is fair
- Absorbs color quickly but fades quickly

Stage 5: -- Excessively Porous Hair

- Breakage
- Over exposure to chemical products
- High alkaline shampoos and over-use of heated styling tools
- Constant shedding when combed or touched
- Elasticity is poor, damaged to loss of cuticle
- Feels extremely fragile.

Coloring African American Natural and Chemically Relaxed Hair

Resistant Hair

Slightly Porous Hair

Average Hair

Overly Porous Hair

Excessively Porous Hair

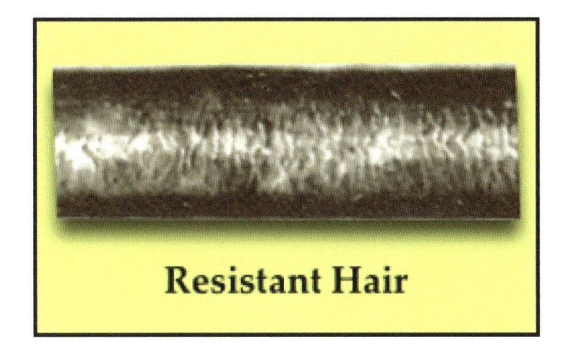

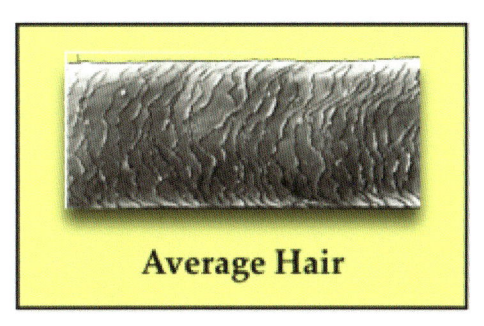

Haircolor Secret

When chemicals are applied to the hair, they completely alter the structure of the strand and increase its porosity. Damage and raised cuticles are the primary issues associated with overly porous hair.

The combination of highlights on a relaxer clients can raise the level of porosity of hair from moderately to over porous. However, porosity can be controlled or reduced throughout the hair with good hair care products that promote moisture and strength in the internal structure of the hair shaft for lasting shine and good elasticity. We will also discuss later in this section other techniques you can use to keep the integrity of the hair.

Next we are going to discuss chemically relaxed hair and see how it is different from Natural hair.

Coloring African American Natural and Chemically Relaxed Hair

Before

After

Natural Hair vs. Chemically Relaxed Hair
How are they Different?

Natural Hair

Natural hair is in the same condition as when it came through the hair follicle. This virgin hair hasn't been treated with chemicals such as relaxers, cold wave, color or any straightening treatment.

Natural hair usually is not very porous because the cuticle has not been lifted as with the use of chemicals. However, natural hair and relaxed hair can both exhibit the same characteristics such as dryness, frizziness and dullness.

By nature, natural African-American hair encounters irregular twisted fibers along the hair shaft, which makes the natural sebum (oil) from the scalp have a very difficult time from flowing from roots to ends.

Coloring African American Natural and Chemically Relaxed Hair

This causes the cuticle of textured (curly or frizzy) hair to become slightly raised at the twist (reverse curl direction) making the hair constantly dry and hard to maintain moisture.

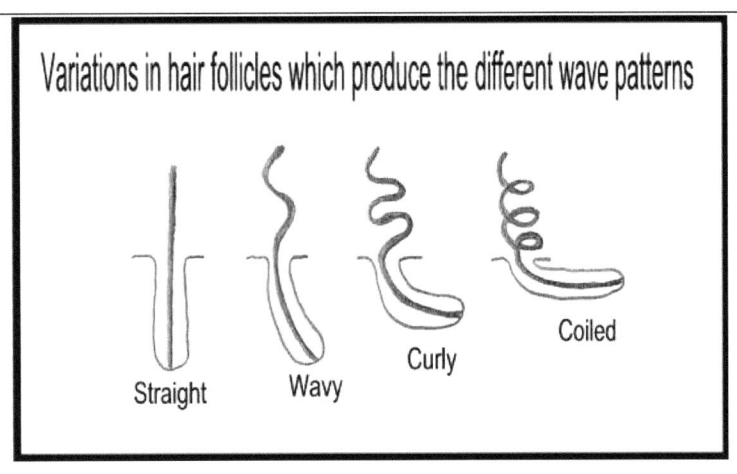

Variations in hair follicles which produce the different wave patterns

Straight — Wavy — Curly — Coiled

Dryness can be related to the decreased ability of sebum (oil) to coat the hair adequately.
Therefore moisturizing maintenance hair styling products are used frequently to add shine and assist with combing and manageability.

Poorly formulated hair care products, heating implements, chlorinated water, salt water and weaves, wearing high stress weaves extensively for a long time without washing the hair, can leave the natural hair strands rough and brittle.

Natural hair usually has different curl patterns within the same head of hair. Every head of hair has its own unique texture of hair regardless of curl type. This explains why selecting the right hair care product, styling aids, and chemical process can be challenging.

Haircolor Secret

Certain textures that are tight, wiry and coarse tend to be resistant to water, chemicals or any other products when trying to penetrate the hair shaft. So by applying the basic law of *"Moisture Attracts Moisture"*, we can apply a moisture-based product onto a damp head of hair instead of a dry head of hair to get better absorption and penetration.

Another characteristic of chemically free textured hair is it has the appearance of looking shorter in contrast when it is thermo relaxed or blow-dried. This is a normal characteristic of natural hair because afro texture hair reverses in curl direction and decreases around the diameter toward the ends of the hair.

Virgin texture has been known to shrink as much as 50% to 70%. This is a normal characteristic that needs to be explained to clients especially those who are thinking about transitioning from a relaxer to natural hair. **The major difference between natural and relaxed hair is called latitude.**

Coloring African American Natural and Chemically Relaxed Hair

Virgin hair has more strength then relaxed hair and it will be able to receive a broader range of coloring services in the salon. For example High-lift and Double Process Blondes will be the services that can be applied to natural texture only rather than relaxed hair.

The key factors in maintaining colored, virgin, textured hair (no relaxer) will be the same as relaxed hair. Keeping the optimum levels of moisture and protein avoids breakage and excessive shedding.

Remember, too strong of peroxide in your formula when coloring or lightening natural hair can badly dissolve or disintegrate the hair cuticle causing severe moisture loss. As stated earlier, natural hair is stronger than relaxed hair but is fragile compared to natural straighter textures.

The curlier the hair the more likely it is to break because it has more **kinks** down the hair shaft, which are called the **weak spots**. It is best to detangle the hair gently **before** combing the hair straight to ensure you don't damage it and pull out the client's hair.

Each of these turns (reverse curl down the hair shaft) represents a weak point or stress point in the hair. That's why careful consideration is still needed just as when doing a client with relaxed hair before performing any coloring services.

Chemically Relaxed Hair

Chemically Relaxed hair is a much different scenario. By simple definition, a hair relaxer makes the hair easier to straighten and manage. It reduces the curl by breaking down the hair strand and chemically altering the internal structure of the texture.
(This will be discussed in detail in a few minutes.)

Most women who decide to get their hair chemically relaxed have curls that are unmanageable and in need of taming. Unlike with natural virgin hair, chemically relaxed hair protein bonds (disulfide bonds) have been broken down to a weaker state called lanthionization. Disulfide bonds have 2 sulfur atoms while the lanthionine bonds have one sulfur atom.

This is why chemically relaxed hair is slightly weaker than natural hair. It is the disulfide bonds that give the hair strength. These protein bonds can only be broken down by chemical process.

Once the disulfide bonds have been weaken, they cannot be reformed. This is why you can't strip out (remove) relaxers. The client either has to grow out their relaxer or have it cut out.

The hair that is **permanently relaxed, not straightened** (that's done with the blow dryer and flat iron) will stay in its fixed relaxed state. Relaxed hair usually needs retouches every 6 to 8 wks. This is where it can become difficult when coloring relaxed hair.

Since relaxed hair is slightly weaker than natural hair, it is best to defer your relaxer color client 8 to 12 weeks before applying the relaxer retouch when highlighting or using demi- permanent or permanent color. However, relaxed hair will respond more quickly to the coloring and lightening process than

Coloring African American Natural and Chemically Relaxed Hair

natural hair, even with the use of lower volume developers. This is due to the high alkaline nature of relaxers causing the cuticle layer to have already been lifted.

Note: The lower the porosity (Stages 1 or 2), the higher the volume of developer. The higher the porosity (Stages 3, 4 & 5) the lower the volume of developer. This allows us to maintain the integrity of the hair for future services and avoid premature color fading.

Porosity in this case is working *for* the colorist by achieving lighter tones with the least amount (Volume) of developer and requiring less processing time. (Generally, 25 to 30 minutes versus the 35 to 40 minutes required for non-relaxed hair unless the hair is fine textured).

Haircolor Secrets

Care for chemically relaxed hair can be significantly more to maintain than natural hair because of the protein bonds having been broken down during the relaxer process. This requires more steps in combating dryness, breakage and maintaining moisture balance.

Compare this to natural hair which just needs a good moisturizing shampoo, conditioner and finishing products, such as defining custard, butters, crèmes and serum for styling with no use of heat.

Natural hair requires little or no heat, giving it a major advantage in keeping the hair in great condition. But styling hair into smooth sleeker styles is much easier on relaxed hair verses natural hair, which needs more heat and humidity resistant products to keep the hair from reverting back into its natural state. Whatever textures you are servicing always take into consideration the amount of heat, products, care and tools it will take to arrive at the finish product in managing color treated hair without damaging the hair.

Variable #5

3 TYPES of CHEMICAL RELAXERS

Introduction

Before we can expect to become proficient at coloring chemically relaxed hair, we must know and understand what types of chemical relaxers are being used in salons today and exactly how they work.

What is important here is to understand the different types of relaxers, what they do to the hair, and how to properly formulate for relaxed hair.

Just as in haircolor, sometimes your client will have a relaxer that you did at your salon or other times your client will have a relaxer that she has had done either in some other salon or even at home.

It is beyond the scope of this book to get into the detailed, deep-science behind how chemical relaxers work, but as haircolorists working on African-American clients, we must have a practical working knowledge of what they are made from and their content in regards to the haircolor service we are about to perform.

For the purposes of this book, we will discuss 3 different types of chemical relaxers, how they differ and then we'll discuss how to perform our haircolor services .

3 Types of Relaxers

The final categories that we need to study are the 3 types of chemical relaxers that you may be working with . These chemical relaxers will fall into one of three different relaxer types:

3 Categories of Relaxer:

1. **Ammonium Thioglycolate (THIO)**

    - Permanent or cold waving solution

2. **"No-Lye" Relaxers**

    - Guanidine Hydroxide
    - Calcium Hydroxide
    - Lithium Hydroxide
    - Potassium Hydroxide

Coloring African American Natural and Chemically Relaxed Hair

3. **"Lye" Relaxers**

    - Sodium Hydroxide

NOTE: Lye and No Lye Relaxers are also known as "Base" or "No Base" Relaxers.

- A "No Base" relaxer is one that does not require the use of an additional base (protective cream) on the scalp prior to the application of the relaxing agent.

- Sodium Hydroxide is considered a "Pure Lye" relaxer and requires the use of a "base" (protective cream) to be applied on the scalp prior to the application of the relaxer.

Types of Relaxers

The technological advances in relaxers have vastly improved since the days of visionary inventor Garrett Augustus Morgan in the 1800's. Today manufacturers have given us more education than ever to get the best results for our clients. We have options to customize our relaxer of choice for situations ranging from itchy dry scalp to color treated hair.

There are many names that describe relaxed hair such as: straightened hair, chemically treated hair, cold wave and the list continue! But despite the various names, we have a common problem among our fellow stylists in fully understanding of how relaxers work, what type of relaxers to use and the correct timing upon application for rinsing.

Most African American women who receive relaxers eventually have breakage or slow growth in growing their hair out. Their only alternative if their hair falls out is to sew in new hair (weave).

Let me be clear the problem is not the relaxer; it's the responsibility of the stylist to choose the right product, strength and technique in order to avoid travesties for the client.

Before & After of a Sodium Hydroxide Relaxer

The Differences Between
Ammonium Thiogylcolate and Hydroxide Relaxers

Ammonium **Thioglycolate** (Thio) is used to straighten as well as curl the hair. The same chemical reaction that puts curl in hair during the permanent wave procedure (perm or cold wave), takes curl out of hair during a chemical straightening procedure.

Thioglycolate relaxers are mildly alkaline, low-pH chemical straighteners.

Like lye and no-lye relaxers, thio formulas also work by breaking disulfide bonds in the hair. These products use ammonium thioglycolate to straighten the hair. These "thio" straightening products have pHs ranging from 6 to 9 and come from the same chemical family as permanents that curl straight hair.

For permanent waves (making curl), the formula is applied and the hair is which has had perm rods in place to produce curls. For straightening curly hair, the product is simply combed through and the hair is smoothed to straighten it and then a neutralizer (hydrogen peroxide solution) is used to "FIX" the hair in its new shape.

Thio relaxers are not compatible with any form of hydroxide relaxer and cannot be applied to hair that has been previously relaxed with lye or no-lye preparations.

Unfortunately, thio relaxers rarely produce impressive straightening results and are extremely hard on African–American hair. Hydroxide relaxers are by far the most popular relaxers used in professional salons today so we will discuss these next.

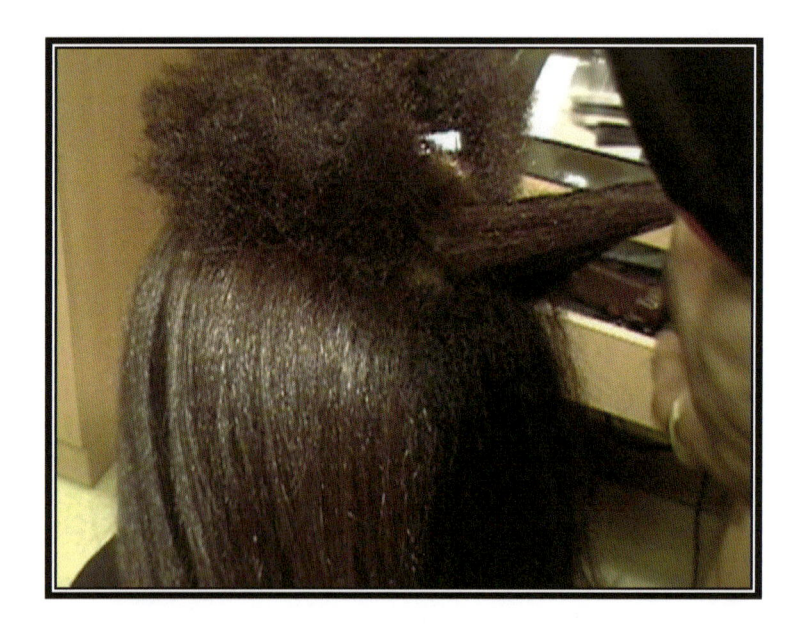

Coloring African American Natural and Chemically Relaxed Hair

Thio relaxers differ from hydroxide relaxers in a few ways.

- The pH of Thio relaxers is typically around 9.6 whereas the pH of hydroxide relaxers is approximately 12 -13.

- The Ammonium Thioglycolate relaxer is often called a **re-arranger**; it is softer and less caustic because of its lower pH. It softens and relaxes tight coils and curls.

- An oxidizing agent like **Hydrogen Peroxide** is used to neutralize Thio relaxers.
(The Neutralizer)

- During the neutralization process of a Thio relaxer, the disulfide bonds that were broken by the relaxing process are reformed thus keeping the hair in its new fixed shape. (Straight or curly)

- The Neutralizer for sodium hydroxide relaxers is an **Acidic Shampoo**. This Shampoo completely stops the action of the relaxer after it is rinsed out. It deescalates the high pH balance that occurs during the relaxing process.

- When using hydroxide relaxers, the broken disulfide bonds are permanently broken and cannot be reformed again. Also, neutralizing/oxidizing agents should not be used with hydroxide relaxers only the Acidic Shampoo as mentioned above.

- In Sodium hydroxide relaxers the active ingredient has a higher pH (12 -13) than Thio relaxers. Both relaxers soften and swell hair fibers. The higher the sodium hydroxide content the higher the pH and the quicker the reaction will take place on the hair.

NOTE:
These two relaxers systems (Thio and Hydroxide) should **never be used interchangeably**. Overlapping these chemicals can cause extreme damage to the hair, and can result in hair loss. The two active ingredients hydroxide and Thio are **incompatible** once overlapped will cause **severe damage and a law suit !**

Hydroxide Relaxers:

Hydroxide relaxers are the most commonly used chemical relaxers in professional salons today. These relaxers include products based on sodium hydroxide, lithium hydroxide, potassium hydroxide and guanidine hydroxide. Hydroxide relaxers can be broken down into two basic formulations: those with lye and those without lye.

The chemical compounds responsible for breaking the hair bonds are the major difference between lye and no-lye formulas.

- **In lye relaxers, this bond-breaking compound is sodium hydroxide.**

- **In no-lye relaxers, the bond-breaking compound is guanidine hydroxide.**

Coloring African American Natural and Chemically Relaxed Hair

Through advertising the general public believes no lye is less harmful than lye relaxers, but the FDA has received many complaints about scalp irritations and breakage related to both relaxers.

No-lye and lye relaxers contain ingredients that work by breaking chemical bonds of the hair, and both can burn the scalp and degrade the hair severely if used incorrectly. Lye relaxers contain sodium hydroxide as the active ingredient. And in "no lye" relaxers, calcium hydroxide and guanidine carbonate are mixed to produce guanidine hydroxide.

Research has discovered that no-lye relaxers have less irritation on the scalp than "lye" sodium hydroxide relaxers, but chemically has the same effect on the hair. The same rules apply for both as far as timing, technique and process when rinsing, neutralizing shampoo and conditioning to ensure safety for the clients

> Furthermore, within each of the two-hydroxide relaxer types **(lye & no-lye)**,
> each type is sold in 3 different strengths **(Mild—Regular—Super)**.
> We will discuss these three different strengths a little later.

Let's take a practical in-depth look at how a relaxer works.

When applied, the relaxer immediately upon contact begins the process of swelling the cuticle layer of the hair so it can enter the cortical layer of the cortex causing irreversible changes. Then it starts to permanently break the cohesive disulfide bonds that hold the bonds together as a cohesive unit causing the natural curl to loosen and become relaxed up to 80% **not straighten.**

If during this process it becomes bone straight, the inner structural damage occurs such as poor elasticity, limp hair, and constant shedding (hair loss). It is at the cortical level (cortex) where change is taking place, that provides strength, elasticity and shape to the hair. Once you go past the stated timing or use the wrong relaxer strength, the damages are past the state of no return. You have to cut the hair!

What is the Practical Difference between "Lye" and "No Lye' relaxers?

There really is not much of a difference between **lye** and **no lye** relaxers in regards to how they work because they all come from the hydroxide family and have highly caustic metallic bases. **The main difference is the scalp comfort that no lye provides for highly sensitive scalps.**

TIP: Although no base relaxers have a thin, oil-like protective cream within the relaxer system to protect the scalp, it is still best to use a base cream around the ears and hairline for added protection.

Coloring African American Natural and Chemically Relaxed Hair

"No-Lye" Hydroxide Relaxers

1. **Guanidine Hydroxide**
2. **Calcium Hydroxide**
3. **Lithium Hydroxide**
4. **Potassium Hydroxide**

NOTE: **Lye and No Lye relaxers are also known as "base" or "no base" relaxers.**

Though no-lye relaxers claim to have no traces of lye (or "caustic soda"), this statement is not entirely true as the guanidine, lithium, and potassium hydroxides are in the same metal hydroxide family as sodium hydroxide.

No Lye relaxers tend to be gentle on the scalp but dryer on the hair.
In contrast, Lye relaxers can be caustic to the scalp if not applied properly but leave the hair with a silkier feel.

One of the trade-offs for using a No-Lye relaxer is Calcium Build-up.

No-lye relaxers (guanidine hydroxide) create hard calcium deposits throughout the hair strands that stick to the hair shaft even after subsequent shampoos. Calcium build-up decreases the hair's ability to absorb moisture leaving the hair appearing thin, dull and lifeless. When the hair becomes dry and brittle, strands of hair are soon to break. This dryness is perhaps the greatest complaint of individuals who use no-lye relaxers.

Yes, no lye relaxers can be continued successfully for long time when using clarifying shampoos, but monitor the density of the hair to avoid thinning of the hair shaft that may occur. No-lye starts out slow but accelerates in strength the longer it stays on the hair, causing the keratin protein within the hair shaft to lose its density over time.

If possible it is best to switch the client over to a mild relaxer depending on hair texture & density to avoid thinness to the hair. But, again monitor your sodium hydroxide relaxers; to see if your client may have to eliminate relaxers altogether and go natural if the situation dictates such a move.

"Lye" Hydroxide Relaxer

- **Sodium Hydroxide:**

Lye relaxers are the preferred chemical relaxer formula of the salon industry.

Coloring African American Natural and Chemically Relaxed Hair

These sodium hydroxide-based relaxers are stronger than no-lye relaxers and are generally formulated at a much higher pH. Lye relaxers are said to be easier on the hair and harder on the scalp. This is because they do not leave drying mineral deposits on the hair like No-lye relaxers do, and so are more likely to leave the hair with a softer, silkier result without further treatments.

The ion metals of the sodium hydroxide relaxer produces a pH of 12.5 – 13.5 which accelerates the lye relaxers to break down the bonds quickly. The speed and accuracy in applying the relaxer is of upmost importance to prevent the sodium relaxer from burning the scalp and over processing.

Note: When applying sodium relaxers, keep the relaxer ¼ away from scalp upon application. During the last 5 min of the processing time, apply the remaining relaxer on the ¼ section that was not relaxed. Remember the new growth is softer at the scalp than the midshaft to the ends of the hair, because the new growth isn't fully keratinized like the other parts of the hair shaft!

Lye relaxers can be caustic to the scalp if not applied properly, but they leave the hair with a silkier feeling than No-Lye relaxers and have no calcium build-up.

Compared to no-lye relaxers, lye relaxers are more likely to provide an acceptable level of disulfide bond breakage that still allows the hair to retain its natural strength and elasticity.

This lower degree of bond breakage tends to produce moderately straight results compared to no-lye relaxers, despite the generally higher pH. Disulfide bond breakage may be reduced in lye relaxers because its chemical aggressiveness tends to put time constraints on the straightening process.

Because they are able to lift the cuticle layers more forcefully and breech protective layers of petroleum base more quickly, lye relaxers must be applied carefully and quickly to avoid damage to the hair and scalp.

When applying color it is best to use no higher than 20-volume peroxide added to your color formula. Also, the stylist should use a mild strength relaxer when following up for a retouch relaxer.

Texturizer

A texturizer is an application technique using a mild hydroxide relaxer to release a strong curl pattern .This technique achieves a softer look that allows the hair to be more manageable and retain its strength.

The outcome or result of each curl depends upon the curl pattern with which you begin. Your assessment of the type of curl pattern – tight curl or kinky - will predetermine the timing, starting point of application (each section of hair has its own curl pattern) and visual observation of how long it should process.

Our tool of choice is a rubber medium width rattail comb in application but with absolutely no smoothing. When you smooth the hair you immediately move the technique into a relaxer, breaking more protein bonds than desired.

Coloring African American Natural and Chemically Relaxed Hair

This technique allows you to apply the product to the hair and visually watch how much you want the curl to be released. Many stylists and clients have misunderstood this service and technique to be only relegated to short hair clients.

The service can benefit medium to long hair clients including relaxer clients transitioning into a texturizer.

Remember it's about technique, timing, and application.

Hot tip: The relaxer process or texturizer will process much faster when larger amounts of product are applied to the new growth or virgin application. Once it starts, you are not in control with the exception of rinsing the product off to avoid scalp burns and over-processing of the hair. (Keep relaxers off the scalp including texturizers).

Summary:

Regardless of what strength of hydroxide relaxer we use, the relaxers swells the hair cuticle as it enters the cortical layer of the hair causing permanent and irreversible changes to the disulfide bonds causing the hair texture to become relaxed (not straight) until the new growth comes in.

Very Important
This is where the problems arise in coloring relaxed hair. If more than 80% of the protein bonds are broken, they will erode the strength and elasticity we need to support our permanent color service.

We can't control the heat reaction that occurs when we apply the relaxer on the hair but we can control the timing and product selection when choosing the proper strength of relaxer to use for the clients texture.

One of the keys in maintaining healthy relaxed hair is deferring the relaxer application to 8-to 12 weeks to avoid overlapping and breakage from the weak points of the irregular curl pattern.

Overlapping

When we reduce the frequency of relaxer application (8 to 12 weeks instead of 6 to 8 weeks) the potential is greatly reduced for over lapping previously relaxed hair or color treated hair and thus avoids scalp issues. You have more new growth to work with at the time of your application.

Application of Relaxer

Your application processing time starts the moment you apply your relaxer. Timing is generally 13 minutes for fine hair, 15 minutes for normal hair, 18 to 20 minutes for coarse hair. If the hair is above normal porosity, give a deep protein moisture treatment to bring into balance the porosity, moisture and strength to the hair shaft, so that you will be able to support the relaxer service upon her next visit. The timing for each individual texture stated above should never be exceeded!

Coloring African American Natural and Chemically Relaxed Hair

The timing for each individual texture receiving a relaxer is a precautionary guideline, the stylist should always keep an eye on the process to see if the relaxer needs to be rinse out before the stated time to avoid breakage. It's imperative that the relaxer be applied in a timely manner finer textures (5minutes) normal (6 minutes) coarse dense hair (8minutes) .

Coloring African American Natural and Chemically Relaxed Hair

Three Strengths of Hydroxide Relaxers
Mild, Regular & Super

The pH of relaxers range from 9.6 to 13.5. The readings of all three are relatively the same, but the concentration of alkali vary among relaxer strengths.

Coloring relaxed hair successfully whether it is no-lye or lye depends on what strength of relaxer is being used. Choosing a milder strength reduces the amount of disulfide bond breakage, allowing the colorist to have more flexibility in permanent coloring and lightening because of the remaining strength and elasticity in the hair shaft. The more protein bonds that are broken in the hair, the more chance of breakage when applying permanent color on the hair.

<u>Caution:</u> Make sure the client does not have any metallic salt products on her hair, such as henna's and some box colors when you are applying either a thio or hydroxide relaxer. This helps you avoid extreme damage or breakage.

Relaxers by nature are high in pH, which causes the cuticle to swell and become distorted regardless of the strength you choose. However, the stronger the relaxer (regular to super) the quicker it will begin attacking the protein bonds in the hair and the scalp.

All strengths of chemical relaxers can and will climb up the pH scale if left beyond prescribed timing. Timing is the only element we control in the equation of relaxing hair. This is where technique takes over in skillfully and quickly applying off the scalp relaxers on new growth only (1/4 from scalp and closer to the scalp during the last few minutes of the process), allowing sufficient time to check if the relaxer SHOULD BE RINSED before the allotted time! Due to porosity and slight changing of texture (because of age, diet, medication) each time you relax the same head of hair the timing changes!

The next challenge is how do I reduce the swelling (porosity) back to its original state? Of course, use the neutralizer shampoo, right? That answer is half right. The pH activity is so high that neutralizing shampoos alone will not fully contract the cuticle layer.

You will need to use a **liquid acidifier** at a pH of 1 to fully reduce the swelling of the cuticle to its former state after using your favorite neutralizer shampoo. The liquid acidifier not only assists in scaling back the cuticle layers but also it gets rid of every speck of relaxer residue that isn't revealed through the neutralizer shampoo! Controlling the porosity is the number one priority in maintaining its elasticity, body and shine.

pH of Chemical Relaxers

The chart below clearly shows the relationship of the three types of chemical relaxers and their average corresponding pH level.

NOTE: Both Lye and No-Lye relaxers are available in 3 different strengths.

Mild—Regular—Super

When the strength of these relaxers move up the pH scale from Mild to Super, so does the speed in which they work and the possible damage to the cuticle layer of the hair if not done properly.

These are key points to consider when doing the haircolor consultation and formulating.

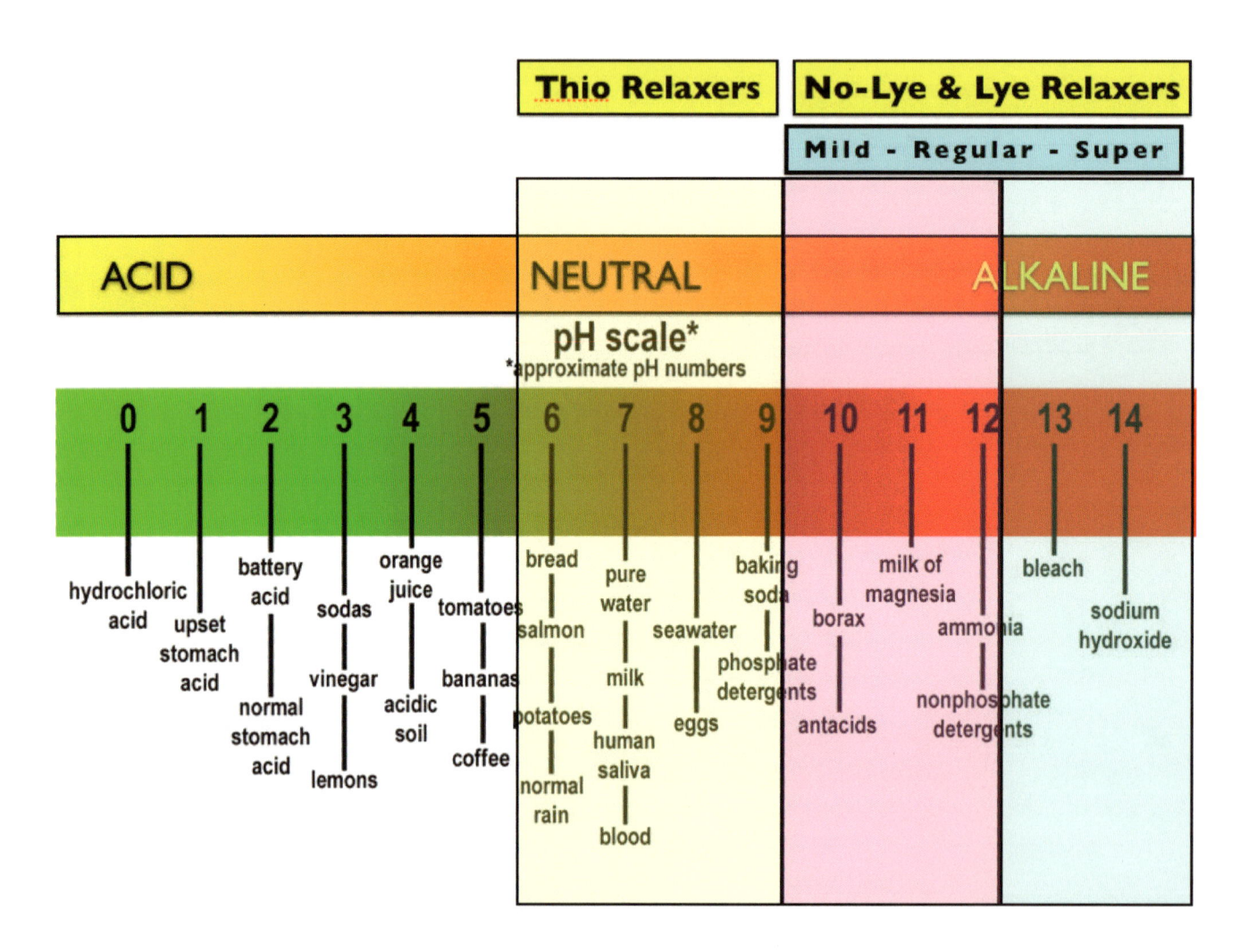

pH	Substance
0	hydrochloric acid
1	upset stomach acid
2	battery acid, normal stomach acid
3	sodas, vinegar
4	orange juice, acidic soil, lemons
5	tomatoes, bananas, coffee
6	bread, salmon, potatoes, normal rain
7	pure water, milk, human saliva, blood
8	seawater, eggs
9	baking soda, phosphate detergents
10	milk of magnesia, borax, antacids
11	ammonia, nonphosphate detergents
12	
13	bleach
14	sodium hydroxide

Thio Relaxers: pH range ~6–9 (Neutral)
No-Lye & Lye Relaxers (Mild - Regular - Super): pH range ~9–14 (Alkaline)

Coloring African American Natural and Chemically Relaxed Hair

Pre-treating Chemically Relaxed Hair for Color

Everything we have shared with you about coloring chemically relaxed hair so far has been important. However, this segment of the book is essential and ongoing in knowing and preparing your clients for highlights or permanent color, This is so your guests can avoid excessive shedding, breakage or just flat out massive hair loss inside your shampoo bowl!

The steps below are proven strategies that have helped us learn how to overcome the obstacle of coloring relaxed hair without severe damage. Hopefully these tips will benefit you and your staff as well.

1. The condition of the hair upon consultation will let you know how well the texture will look after the color application. This is the determining factor, if you should color the hair or prescribe a treatment.

2. Highly textured (very curly/kinky) and relaxed hair are naturally dry and require heavy dosages of moisture. Steam treatments are an excellent choice in preparing hair for a future color service.

3. The golden rule is to color the relaxed hair, never relax the color treated hair. Many times a first time client will request a haircolor service after she has just relaxed her hair at home.

4. Be thorough in your consultation. In this case apply liquid protein moisturizing conditioning treatments periodically until her next relaxer touchup. Allow 7 to 14 days to elapse before you apply permanent haircolor or highlights. This way you are able to reduce the porosity level, improve elasticity and control how much fiber you need to leave in the hair, when you perform the relaxer service. Only then will you be able to successfully apply the permanent color or highlight service for the client.

5. If hair is damaged and porous, reshape the hair and provide a Protein moisturizing treatment. Then start slowly with a demi permanent to see if the hair can withstand peroxide without shedding or getting dry hair or scalp. Then work your way up to permanent color or highlights.

Coloring African American Natural and Chemically Relaxed Hair

6. Relaxer clients getting haircolor should never have their hair relaxed to the full ratio of 80%. It should be around 60 to 70 percent, leaving enough fiber to withstand tone on tone (base color then highlights) or permanent hair color.

7. Explain the aftercare maintenance commitment to your clients so they know what they should do as far as buying maintenance hair care products, daily regime and other accessories that will maintain their moisture levels.

8. If clients have been getting relaxers every 6 weeks, start extending their relaxers 8 to 12 weeks so their hair will be able support the permanent color and highlight services.

Clients who desire much lighter levels of color should be consulted with the option of transitioning to texturizers or natural hair to better be able to receive that service without breakage to their hair.

Coloring African American Natural and Chemically Relaxed Hair

Let's Bring it All Together

What is the Texture (Diameter of each strand) is the hair?

- Fine
- Medium
- Coarse

What texture (curl formation) does my client have?

- Wavy
- Curly
- Kinky

What is the hair's density (quantity per square inch of scalp)?

- Fine
- Medium
- Thick

What "Stage of Porosity" is the hair?

1. Resistant
2. Slightly Porous
3. Normal Porosity
4. Overly Porous
5. Excessively Porous Hair

Has the hair been Chemically Relaxed? If so, What TYPE of Relaxer was done?

- **Ammonium Thioglycolate (THIO)**
- **"No-Lye" Relaxers**
- **"Lye" Relaxers**

These are the questions that need to be repetitively asked to each client in locating what her curl type is and know the condition of the hair in order to prescribe a customized service and products for her specific texture.

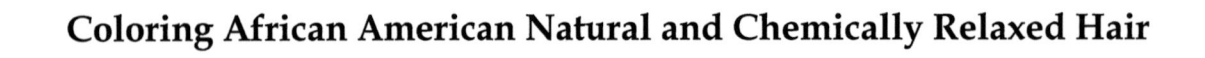

Coloring African American Natural and Chemically Relaxed Hair

Understanding the Formulation Charts

This page gives you the key to better understand how to use the following charts and also it will give you a better idea as to how we have arrived at the formulas in which we will give to you later in this book.

> **Please Note:** The formulas that are being recommended to you are to be used only as **"Guidelines"** for you to follow. Keep in mind that it is your responsibility to assess the hair's condition, texture, porosity and density of each client and adjust these formulas, as needed for your finial desired results.

Have fun with the formulas and refer to the charts as often as needed. They will save you time and hopefully help take your formulation knowledge to the next level!

Haircolor Products

Ro = Red Orange: Also, a Red Orange base mixed with Red concentrate works great when wanting to create strong lasting reds.

Bv = Blue Violet: A Blue Violet base in permanent color helps to control warmth when lifting 2 to 4 levels on dark hair.

RC= Red Concentrate: Red Concentrate can be mixed into permanent or demi color formulations to intensify the red formula. (No need to add extra developer, which would only dilute the concentration.)

GC = Gold Concentrate: This concentrate can be mixed into permanent or demi color formulas to intensify warmth. (No added developer needed, so you don't dilute the concentration.)

Grc = Green Concentrate: This can be mixed into permanent or demi color formula to help subdue the unwanted warmth that will be produced when lightening. (No added developer needed, so you don't dilute the concentrate.)

NOTE: All of the formulas on the charts refer to using permanent haircolor and 20-Volume developer unless noted otherwise **The word "DEMI" or some similar notation will indicate a change in which product to use.**

Lighteners (Bleaches)

Lightener crème: - Lightening crème is also called Blonding booster, lightening oil etc. Every manufacturer has one in their haircolor line. These products have higher ammonia content than the rest of the colors in the line and they usually can be used by it self or mixed into your formula to increase lightening action.

Coloring African American Natural and Chemically Relaxed Hair

Note: You will see a recommendation in our charts using 5 inches of lightening crème mixed with powder lightener when applying highlights. However this amount is variable to as much as 1 pt depending on porosity and texture of the client. By increasing the measure of crème lightner, with powder lightner you buffer the strength of the powder lightner to create beautiful honey highlights without the use of a toner on virging hair!

Extra lightning crème = Xtra lightening crème has a higher ammonia content than lightening crème. This would be a mild bleach that could be in crème or oil form. It can be used by itself as an on-the-scalp lightener or in your formula to provide slightly more aggressive lift than that of regular lightening crème.

Powder Bleach (P/B) - Powder bleach can't be used on a scalp.
It is only used for off the scalp lightening or off the scalp color removal.

Note: If your client natural base is a level 2 darkest brown. But, they desire for you to lift their base color lighter than 5 levels, it is best to use a permanent color to lift their natural base no more than 2 levels. Then you can apply highlights over the new base color by using mild lightener to give the client their desired level of lightness. Do not try to lift the base more than 2 levels or your results will create uncontrollable warm tones (usually orange).

~Levels 7,8,9 in the charts are formulated using a technique called "Tone on Tone" Its when you change the natural haircolor and then you add highlights.

Demi Permanent Color

Note: On some of the charts you will see that I recommend mixing Lightening crème with demi permanent color. I do this to give slight lift for deeper richer tonality.

N/R = Not Recommended: It is our advice that this color service should not be performed, is not necessary or should not be attempted because given the current state of the hair, it could cause breakage.

Developers

10vol- 10 Volume developer: should be use for deposit-only for toning, glazing highlights.

20vol– 20 Volume developer: is used for lift and deposit for relaxed hair. Higher volumes of developers are not recommended for use on chemically relaxed hair.

25vol-25 Volume developer: should only be used on natural hair, **NOT** chemically relaxed hair. If you don't have 25 vol. in your dispensary, you can create it by mixing 20 vol. & 30 vol. in equal parts. **Note:** 25 Volume is great for use on natural coarse, dense hair and for better penetration on resistant gray hair.

Coloring African American Natural and Chemically Relaxed Hair

Mixing Ratios

Pt.=Parts - The term **"Parts"** is used for universal purposes because every one doesn't use grams or ounces. So for easy formulation, I use "parts" which should be located on your color tube.

Each product manufacturer has it's own individual size tube so "parts" will vary because of the size of the tube.
- ½ Pt – equals 15 grams or ½ oz
- 1Pt- equals 30 grams or 1oz
- 1/3Pt- 8 grams or .33 oz

Standard ratios for primary tones are 1-1/2 part to 1/3 or 1/2 part secondary tone.

Coloring African American Natural and Chemically Relaxed Hair

Haircolor Selector Grids and Hair Classification Charts

In this next section of the book we will give you two groups of charts:

    Group 1 – Natural Curl Texture Charts
    Group 2 – Chemically Relaxed Texture Charts

At the beginning of each group of charts you will find the Grids below.

Haircolor Selector Grids

African American Natural Hair Types
Types of Natural Curl Texture

KEY	Wavy	Curly	Kinky
Stage 1	NT-1	NT-6	NT-11
Stage 2	NT-2	NT-7	NT-12
Stage 3	NT-3	NT-8	NT-13
Stage 4	NT-4	NT-9	NT-14
Stage 5	NT-5	NT-10	NT-15

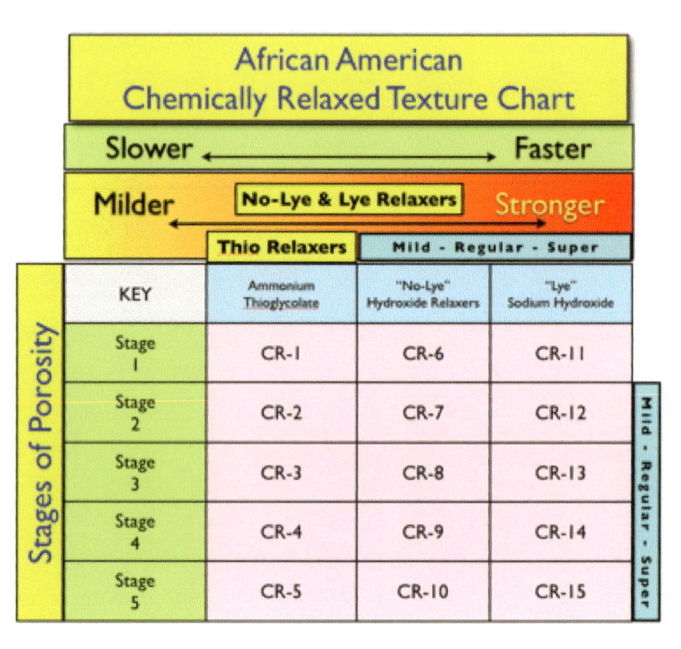

Stages of Porosity

African American Chemically Relaxed Texture Chart

Slower ←→ Faster
Milder — No-Lye & Lye Relaxers — Stronger
Thio Relaxers | Mild - Regular - Super

KEY	Ammonium Thioglycolate	"No-Lye" Hydroxide Relaxers	"Lye" Sodium Hydroxide
Stage 1	CR-1	CR-6	CR-11
Stage 2	CR-2	CR-7	CR-12
Stage 3	CR-3	CR-8	CR-13
Stage 4	CR-4	CR-9	CR-14
Stage 5	CR-5	CR-10	CR-15

Stages of Porosity | Mild - Regular - Super

Within each grid you will see **15 boxes** that will represent the 15 charts in that group.

Such as "NT-1 or CR-8"

"**NT**" stands for **NATURAL TEXTURE**, "**CR**" stands for **CHEMICALLY RELAXED**

The "**Number**" after these letters indicates which **HAIR CLASSIFICATION CHART** you need to go to, to find the formulas.

Coloring African American Natural and Chemically Relaxed Hair

Hair Classification Charts

Hair Classification   NT-1

Desired Color	Pre-Lightening Necessary	Product Category	Notes
Blondes			
Light Blonde Level 9	20 vol / pwdr/ 3"xtra lightener crème	Demi 10g+10bv	Do not exceed 10 mins.
Med. Blonde Level 7-8	10 vol/ pwdr/ 5'lightnr crème	Demi 8g+10n	10n helps/ tone hair to soft blonde/ No brassiness
Dark Blonde Level 6	N/R	6bv +6g+1pt xtra-lightg crem+25vol.	Add 1/3 pt 6g to formula
Reds			
Light Red Level 7-8-9	10vl pwdr/creme	Demi 10g+ rc 10vl	Use 10vol because of porosity issues
Med. Red Level 5-6	N/R	6g+rc +super xlc 25vol	Add 1pt xlc for Added lift
Dark Red Level 3-4	N/R	4ro + rc 25vol	Rc creates a richer lasting red.
Brunettes			
Light Brown Level 5-6	N/R	10n +3" grc + 25vol	Add ¼ super xlc /Grc to control warmth
Med. Brown Level 4-5	N/R	8n+ grc +1/4pt lightnr crem + 25vl	Add 3" to grc to control warmth
Dark Brown Level 2-3	N/R	4g +25vol	20vol to create warmth/in Dk brn

Once you have found the appropriate **Hair Classification Chart**, all you have to do is look at the first column and select your **DESIRED COLOR**, then read the directions to the right of that color.

The second column labeled **"Pre-Lightening Necessary"** will indicate if you will need to per-lighten or not in order to achieve the desired color. If pre-lightening is needed, you will find our suggested product. If Pre-Lightening is not necessary, it will say **"N/R"**
for **Not Recommended** or **Not Necessary**.

The third column will give you the **Product Category** and **Formulation Suggestion** to achieve that desired color.

Please Remember, these are only **SUGGESTED FORMULATIONS**, you must assess if you will need to alter these formulas in any way dependent upon your particular clients needs.

And in the last column, you will find side **NOTES** that will help in the process of the formulation.

NOTE: On a few charts like **CR-1, CR-6 & CR-11**, you will see **N/R** in all of the boxes.
This simply means that these charts are irrelevant because once a client has had a chemical relaxer there is no way that she could still have Stage-1 porosity.

Coloring African American Natural and Chemically Relaxed Hair

Following are Step-By-Step diagrams showing how to use these grids and charts

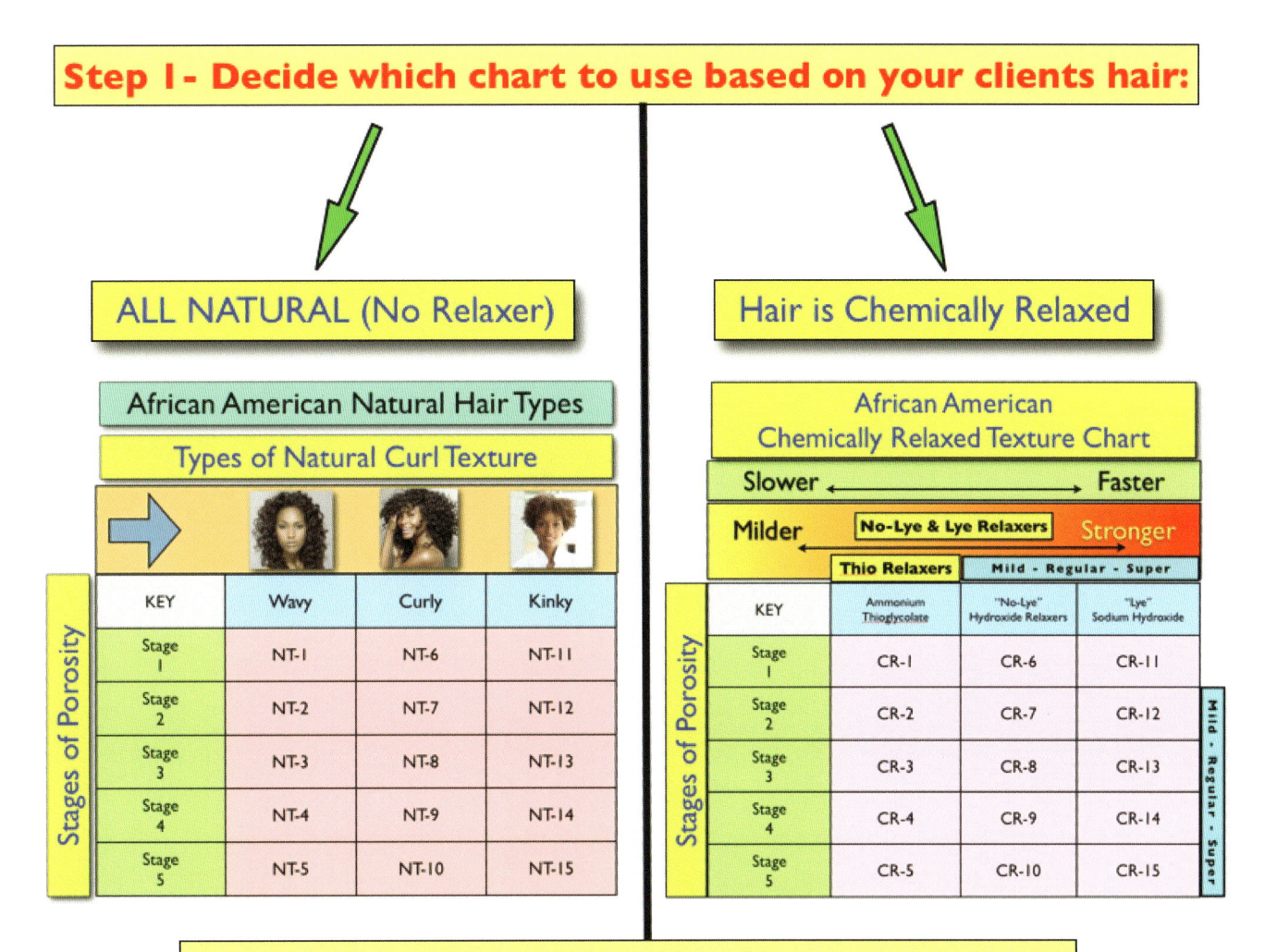

Step 1- Decide which chart to use based on your clients hair:

ALL NATURAL (No Relaxer)

African American Natural Hair Types

Types of Natural Curl Texture

KEY	Wavy	Curly	Kinky
Stage 1	NT-1	NT-6	NT-11
Stage 2	NT-2	NT-7	NT-12
Stage 3	NT-3	NT-8	NT-13
Stage 4	NT-4	NT-9	NT-14
Stage 5	NT-5	NT-10	NT-15

Stages of Porosity

Hair is Chemically Relaxed

African American Chemically Relaxed Texture Chart

Slower → Faster
Milder — No-Lye & Lye Relaxers — Stronger
Thio Relaxers | Mild - Regular - Super

KEY	Ammonium Thioglycolate	"No-Lye" Hydroxide Relaxers	"Lye" Sodium Hydroxide
Stage 1	CR-1	CR-6	CR-11
Stage 2	CR-2	CR-7	CR-12
Stage 3	CR-3	CR-8	CR-13
Stage 4	CR-4	CR-9	CR-14
Stage 5	CR-5	CR-10	CR-15

Stages of Porosity | Mild - Regular - Super

Step 2- Go to Corresponding Chart in the Book

Coloring African American Natural and Chemically Relaxed Hair

ALL NATURAL (No Relaxer)

Step 2 - Select Stage of Porosity and Type of Curl

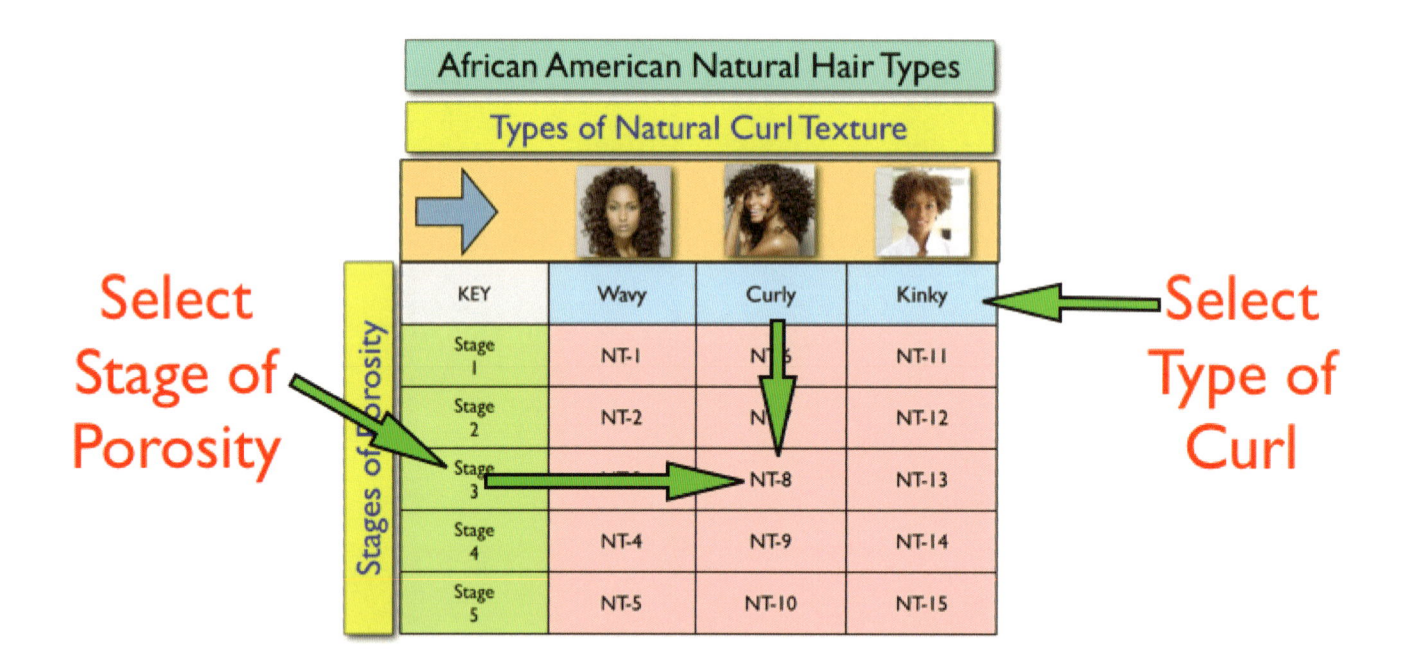

African American Natural Hair Types

Types of Natural Curl Texture

KEY	Wavy	Curly	Kinky
Stage 1	NT-1	NT-6	NT-11
Stage 2	NT-2	NT-7	NT-12
Stage 3	NT-3	NT-8	NT-13
Stage 4	NT-4	NT-9	NT-14
Stage 5	NT-5	NT-10	NT-15

Select Stage of Porosity ← → *Select Type of Curl*

Step 3 - Go to Corresponding Chart in Box
Example: Chart "NT-8"

Coloring African American Natural and Chemically Relaxed Hair

Hair is Chemically Relaxed

Step 2-Select Stage of Porosity and Type of Type of Chemical Relaxer

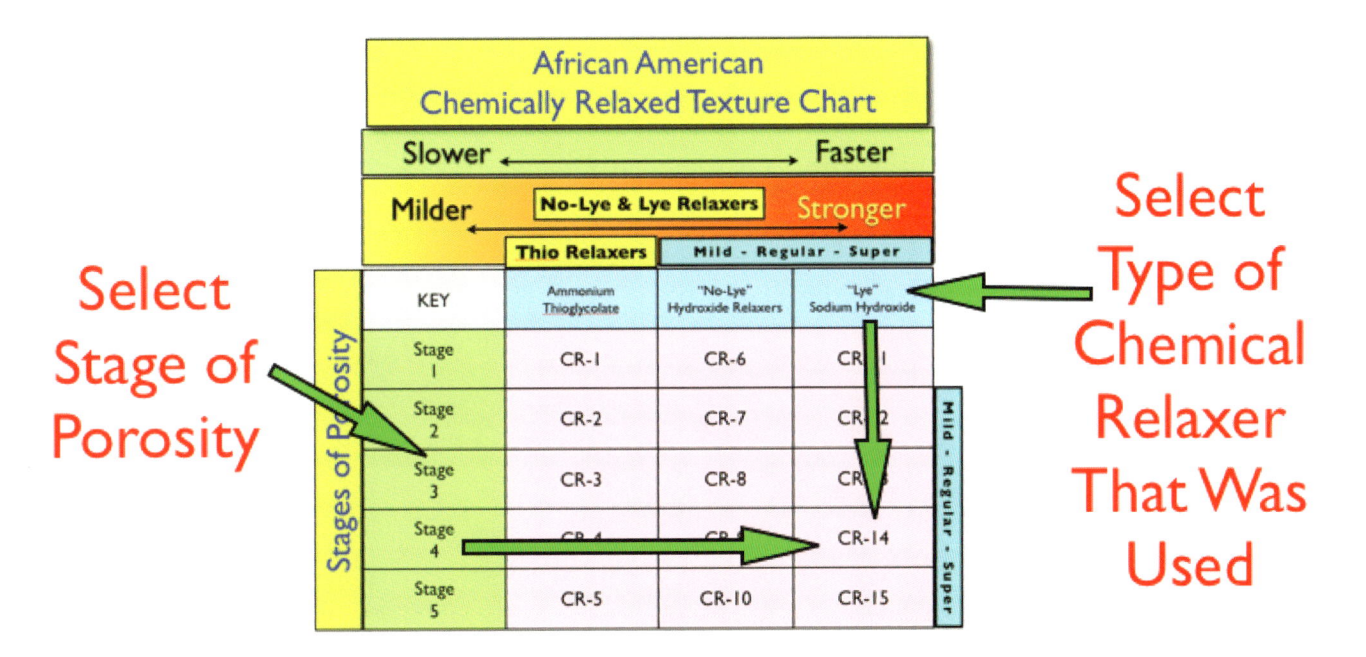

African American Chemically Relaxed Texture Chart

Slower ← → Faster

Milder — No-Lye & Lye Relaxers — Stronger

Thio Relaxers | Mild - Regular - Super

KEY	Ammonium Thioglycolate	"No-Lye" Hydroxide Relaxers	"Lye" Sodium Hydroxide
Stage 1	CR-1	CR-6	CR-11
Stage 2	CR-2	CR-7	CR-12
Stage 3	CR-3	CR-8	CR-13
Stage 4	CR-4	CR-9	CR-14
Stage 5	CR-5	CR-10	CR-15

Select Stage of Porosity

Select Type of Chemical Relaxer That Was Used

**Step 3-Go to Corresponding Chart in Box
Example: Chart "CR-14"**

Coloring African American Natural and Chemically Relaxed Hair

Step 4 - When you find the Corresponding Chart, Select your Desired End Result and find the Suggested Formula

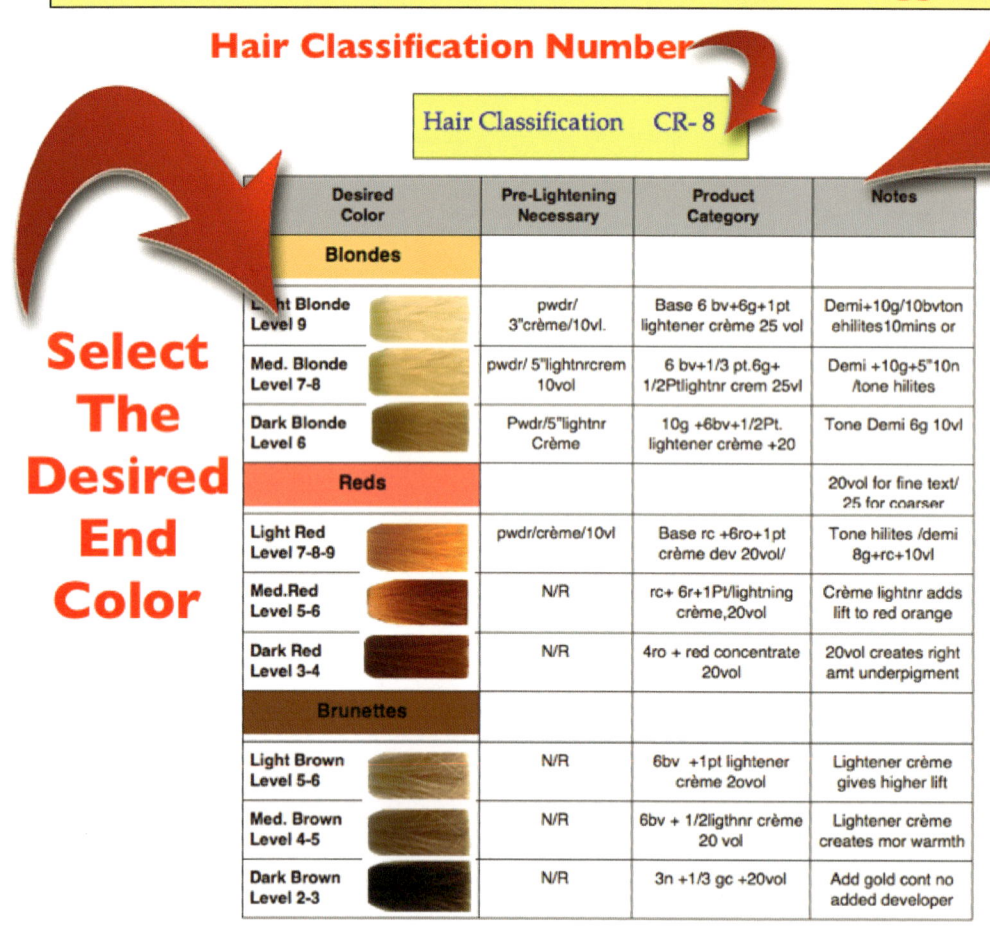

Hair Classification Number

Hair Classification CR-8

Select The Desired End Color

Find Suggested Formula & Notes

Note: Alter the Formula as needed for your Client

Desired Color	Pre-Lightening Necessary	Product Category	Notes
Blondes			
Light Blonde Level 9	pwdr/ 3"crème/10vl.	Base 6 bv+6g+1pt lightener crème 25 vol	Demi+10g/10bvton ehilites10mins or
Med. Blonde Level 7-8	pwdr/ 5"lightnrcrem 10vol	6 bv+1/3 pt.6g+ 1/2Ptlightnr crem 25vl	Demi +10g+5"10n /tone hilites
Dark Blonde Level 6	Pwdr/5"lightnr Crème	10g +6bv+1/2Pt. lightener crème +20	Tone Demi 6g 10vl
Reds			20vol for fine text/ 25 for coarser
Light Red Level 7-8-9	pwdr/crème/10vl	Base rc +6ro+1pt crème dev 20vol/	Tone hilites /demi 8g+rc+10vl
Med. Red Level 5-6	N/R	rc+ 6r+1Pt/lightning crème,20vol	Crème lightnr adds lift to red orange
Dark Red Level 3-4	N/R	4ro + red concentrate 20vol	20vol creates right amt underpigment
Brunettes			
Light Brown Level 5-6	N/R	6bv +1pt lightener crème 2ovol	Lightener crème gives higher lift
Med. Brown Level 4-5	N/R	6bv + 1/2ligthnr crème 20 vol	Lightener crème creates mor warmth
Dark Brown Level 2-3	N/R	3n +1/3 gc +20vol	Add gold cont no added developer

Coloring African American Natural and Chemically Relaxed Hair

Group 1 – Natural Curl Texture Charts

African American Natural Hair Types

Types of Natural Curl Texture

KEY	Wavy	Curly	Kinky
Stage 1	NT-1	NT-6	NT-11
Stage 2	NT-2	NT-7	NT-12
Stage 3	NT-3	NT-8	NT-13
Stage 4	NT-4	NT-9	NT-14
Stage 5	NT-5	NT-10	NT-15

Stages of Porosity

Coloring African American Natural and Chemically Relaxed Hair

Hair Classification   NT-1

Desired Color	Pre-Lightening Necessary	Product Category	Notes
Blondes			
Light Blonde Level 9	20 vol / pwdr/ 3"xtra lightener crème	Demi 10g+10bv	Do not exceed 10 mins.
Med. Blonde Level 7-8	10 vol/ pwdr/ 5'lightnr crème	Demi 8g+10n	10n helps/ tone hair to soft blonde/ No brassiness
Dark Blonde Level 6	N/R	6bv +6g+1pt xtra-lightg crem+25vol.	Add 1/3 pt 6g to formula
Reds			
Light Red Level 7-8-9	10vl pwdr/creme	Demi 10g+ rc 10vl	Use 10vol because of porosity issues
Med. Red Level 5-6	N/R	6g+rc +super xlc 25vol	Add 1pt xlc for Added lift
Dark Red Level 3-4	N/R	4ro + rc 25vol	Rc creates a richer lasting red.
Brunettes			
Light Brown Level 5-6	N/R	10n +3" grc + 25vol	Add ¼ super xlc /Grc to control warmth
Med. Brown Level 4-5	N/R	8n+ grc +1/4pt lightnr crem + 25vl	Add 3" to grc to control warmth
Dark Brown Level 2-3	N/R	4g +25vol	20vol to create warmth/in Dk brn

Copyright © 2007-2014 by David Velasco: All Rights Reserved : www.Haircolortradesecrets.com

Coloring African American Natural and Chemically Relaxed Hair

Hair Classification   NT-2

Desired Color	Pre-Lightening Necessary	Product Category	Notes
Blondes			
Light Blonde Level 9	20vol / pwdr/ 3" xlc/roots to ends	Demi 10g+10bv+10vl	Equal parts Do not exceed 10mins
Med. Blonde Level 7-8	20vol/pwdr/5"crem lightner	Demi 8g+10n +10vl	1/3pt 10n decrease brassy warmth
Dark Blonde Level 6	N/R	6bv +6g+1pt xtra lightnrcrem25vol.	Add 1/3 part 6g to formula
Reds			
Light Red Level 7-8-9	10vl pwdr/2"creme	Demi 6ro+6g+ (5",rc/noxtra devlp)	Use 10vol for demi for deposit only
Med. Red Level 5-6	N/R	6g+rc + xlc 25vol	Add1/2 xlc for Added lift
Dark Red Level 3-4	N/R	4ro + rc 25vol	1/3pt, Rc creates richer red and longer lasting
Brunettes			
Light Brown Level 5-6	N/R	10n +3" grc + 25vol	Add ¼ super xlc /Grc to control warmth
Med. Brown Level 4-5	N/R	8n+2"grc+25vl	Add grc to control warmth/
Dark Brown Level 2-3	N/R	Demi 4g +25vol	20vol to create warmth in Dk brown

Copyright © 2007-2014 by David Velasco: All Rights Reserved : www.Haircolortradesecrets.com

Coloring African American Natural and Chemically Relaxed Hair

Hair Classification   NT-3

Desired Color	Pre-Lightening Necessary	Product Category	Notes
Blondes			
Light Blonde Level 9	20vl/pwdr/ 5" lightener crème	Demi 10g+ 10bv	Do not exceed 10mins
Med. Blonde Level 7-8	20vol/pwdr/crem lightener 5inches	Demi 8g+10n	1/3pt10n helps to soften tone
Dark Blonde Level 6	N/R	6bv+6g+1Pt xlc + 25vol.	25 vol for coarser hair 20 vol for finer texture
Reds			
Light Red Level 7-8-9	10vl pwdr/ 2inches lightning crème	Demi 10g+ rc 10vl	Use 10vol for demi no lift tone only.
Med. Red Level 5-6	N/R	6g+rc + xlc lightnr+ 25vol	Add 1/2 xlc added lift Red orange stage.
Dark Red Level 3-4	N/R	4ro + rc 25vol	1/3 rc adds richer lasting red.
Brunettes			
Light Brown Level 5-6	N/R	10n + 10g + 25vol	Add ¼ lightening crème for added lift
Med. Brown Level 4-5	N/R	8n +8g 25vol	Add 1/3 8g no added developer
Dark Brown Level 2-3	N/R	4g + 20vol	20vol for lift create warm pigment & deposit for richer color

Coloring African American Natural and Chemically Relaxed Hair

Hair Classification   NT-4

Desired Color	Pre-Lightening Necessary	Product Category	Notes
Blondes			
Light Blonde Level 9	N/R	N/R	N/R
Med. Blonde Level 7-8	N/R	N/R	N/R
Dark Blonde Level 6	N/R	N/R	N/R
Reds			
Light Red Level 7-8-9	N/R	N/R	N/R
Med. Red Level 5-6	N/R	N/R	N/R
Dark Red Level 3-4	N/R	4ro rc +10vol	Use Demi / because of porosity issues
Brunettes			
Light Brown Level 5-6	N/R	N/R	N/R
Med. Brown Level 4-5	N/R	N/R	N/R
Dark Brown Level 2-3	N/R	4g + 1/3pt gc 10vol	Keep 10-vol to create Dark warm brown

Copyright © 2007-2014 by David Velasco: All Rights Reserved : www.Haircolortradesecrets.com

Coloring African American Natural and Chemically Relaxed Hair

Hair Classification   NT-5

Desired Color	Pre-Lightening Necessary	Product Category	Notes
Blondes			
Light Blonde Level 9	N/R	N/R	Treatment / reshape hair damage
Med. Blonde Level 7-8	N/R	N/R	Treatment / reshape hair damage
Dark Blonde Level 6	N/R	N/R	Treatment / reshape hair damage
Reds			
Light Red Level 7-8-9		N/R	Treatment / reshape hair damage
Med. Red Level 5-6	N/R	N/R	Treatment / reshape hair damage
Dark Red Level 3-4	N/R	Semi color red with gold base	Keep formula warm so the ends won't turn dark
Brunettes			
Light Brown Level 5-6	N/R	N/R	Treatment / reshape hair damage
Med. Brown Level 4-5	N/R	N/R	Treatment / reshape hair damage
Dark Brown Level 2-3	N/R	Semi-color brown with warm base	Use warm base /because hair is over-porous

Coloring African American Natural and Chemically Relaxed Hair

Hair Classification NT-6

Desired Color	Pre-Lightening Necessary	Product Category	Notes
Blondes			
Light Blonde Level 9	20vol / pwdr/ 3" xlc	Demi 10g+ 10bv	Do not exceed 10mins
Med. Blonde Level 7-8	10vol/pwdr/ 5"lightnr crème	demi 8g+10n	10n helps/ tone hair to soften tone
Dark Blonde Level 6	N/R	6bv +6g+1pt xtra lightener crème+ 25vol.	6bv controls warmth
Reds			
Light Red Level 7-8-9	10vl pwdr/creme	Demi 10g+ rc 10vl	Use 10vol for deposit only
Med. Red Level 5-6	N/R	6g+rc + xlc 25vol	Add 1pt xlc for added lift
Dark Red Level 3-4	N/R	4ro + rc 25vol	1/3rc gives richer lasting red.
Brunettes			
Light Brown Level 5-6	N/R	10n +3" gc + 25vol	Add ¼ xlc /GC to control warmth
Med. Brown Level 4-5	N/R	8n+ 2"gc + 25vol	Add grc to control warmth
Dark Brown Level 2-3	N/R	4g+ 25vol	20vol to create warmth

Copyright © 2007-2014 by David Velasco: All Rights Reserved : www.Haircolortradesecrets.com

Coloring African American Natural and Chemically Relaxed Hair

Hair Classification NT-7

Desired Color	Pre-Lightening Necessary	Product Category	Notes
Blondes			
Light Blonde Level 9	20vol / pwdr/ 2" xlc	Demi 10g+ 10bv	Do not exceed 10mins
Med. Blonde Level 7-8	20vol/pwdr/ 5"crem lightener	Demi 8g+10n	10n helps/ tone hair to soft blond /no brassiness
Dark Blonde Level 6	N/R	6bv +1pt xtra lightnrcrem25vol.	Add 1/2 part 6g to formula
Reds			
Light Red Level 7-8-9	10vl pwdr/creme	Demi 10g+ rc 10vl	Use 10vol for deposit only
Med. Red Level 5-6	N/R	6g+rc + xlc 25vol	Add 1pt xlc for added lift to red orange
Dark Red Level 3-4	N/R	4ro + rc 25vol	1/3 Pt rc adds richer lasting red.
Brunettes	N/R		
Light Brown Level 5-6	N/R	10n +3" gc + 25vol	Add 1/2pt xlc /GC to control warmth
Med. Brown Level 4-5	N/R	8n+ 2"'gc +1/2pt lightnr crem 25vol	Add grc to control warmth
Dark Brown Level 2-3	N/R	4g +20vol	20vol to create warm Dk brown

Copyright © 2007-2014 by David Velasco: All Rights Reserved : www.HaircolortradeSecrets.com

Coloring African American Natural and Chemically Relaxed Hair

Hair Classification   NT-8

Desired Color	Pre-Lightening Necessary	Product Category	Notes
Blondes			
Light Blonde Level 9	20vl/pwdr/ 3" lightener crème	Demi 10g+ 10bv	Do not exceed 10mins
Med. Blonde Level 7-8	20vol/pwdr/ Crème lightener 5"	Demi 8g+10n	1/3pt10n helps/ tone hair to soft blond
Dark Blonde Level 6	N/R	6bv+1/3pt6g+1pt xtraligthnr crème	25 vol for coarser hair 20 vol for finer texture
Reds			
Light Red Level 7-8-9	10vl pwdr/ 2inches lightning crème	Demi 10g+ 1/3 rc 10vl, no add dev	Use 10vol for demi no lift tone only.
Med. Red Level 5-6	N/R	6g+rc + xlc lightner+ 25vol	Add xlc 1 exta added lift to red orange
Dark Red Level 3-4	N/R	4ro + rc 25vol	rc creates richer tone longer lasting red.
Brunettes			
Light Brown Level 5-6	N/R	10n + 3"grc + 25vol	Add ¼Pt lightening crème for added lift
Med. Brown Level 4-5	N/R	8n +2"grc+ 25vol	Add2"grc no added devlp/control warmth
Dark Brown Level 2-3	N/R	4g+ 20vol	20vol for lift create warm Dk Bk

Copyright © 2007-2014 by David Velasco: All Rights Reserved : www.Haircolortradesecrets.com

Coloring African American Natural and Chemically Relaxed Hair

Hair Classification   NT-9

Desired Color	Pre-Lightening Necessary	Product Category	Notes
Blondes			
Light Blonde Level 9	N/R	N/R	N/R
Med. Blonde Level 7-8	N/R	N/R	N/R
Dark Blonde Level 6	N/R	N/R	N/R
Reds			
Light Red Level 7-8-9	N/R	N/R	N/R
Med. Red Level 5-6	N/R	N/R	N/R
Dark Red Level 3-4	N/R	4ro + rc +10vol	Use Demi for porosity issues
Brunettes			
Light Brown Level 5-6	N/R	N/R	N/R
Med. Brown Level 4-5	N/R	N/R	N/R
Dark Brown Level 2-3	N/R	4g +1/3pt+ 10vol	keep vol at 10vl for porosity issues

Coloring African American Natural and Chemically Relaxed Hair

Hair Classification   NT-10

Desired Color	Pre-Lightening	Product Category	Notes
Blondes			
Light Blonde Level 9	N/R	N/R	Treatment / reshape hair damage
Med. Blonde Level 7-8	N/R	N/R	Treatment / reshape hair damage
Dark Blonde Level 6	N/R	N/R	Treatment / reshape hair damage
Reds			
Light Red Level 7-8-9		N/R	Treatment / reshape hair damage
Med. Red Level 5-6	N/R	N/R	Treatment / reshape hair damage
Dark Red Level 3-4	N/R	Semi-color red with gold base	Keep formula warm so the ends won't turn dark
Brunettes			
Light Brown Level 5-6	N/R	N/R	Treatment / reshape hair damage
Med. Brown Level 4-5	N/R	N/R	Treatment / reshape hair damage
Dark Brown Level 2-3	N/R	Semi-color Brown with warm base	Use warm base /because hair is over-porous

Coloring African American Natural and Chemically Relaxed Hair

Hair Classification   NT-11

Desired Color	Pre-Lightening Necessary	Product Category	Notes
Blondes			
Light Blonde Level 9	20vol / pwdr/ 3"lightnrcreme	Demi 10g+ 10bv	Do not exceed 10mins
Med. Blonde Level 7-8	20vol/pwdr/5"light nrcreme	Demi 8g+10n	10n helps/ tone hair to soft blond /no
Dark Blonde Level 6	N/R	6bv +6g+1pt xtra lightener crème+ 25vol.	Add 1/2 part 6g to formula
Reds			
Light Red Level 7-8-9	10vl pwdr/creme	Demi 10g+ rc 10vl	Deposit only color
Med. Red Level 5-6	N/R	6g+rc + xlc 25vol	Add 1pt xlc for added lift red orange
Dark Red Level 3-4	N/R	4ro + rc 25vol	.
Brunettes			
Light Brown Level 5-6	N/R	10n + 2" grc + 25vol	Add 1/2 s xlc /GrC to control warmth
Med. Brown Level 4-5	N/R	8n+1/4pt xlc + 25vol	8n to control warmth
Dark Brown Level 2-3	N/R	4g+ 25vol	20vol to create warm dark brown

Coloring African American Natural and Chemically Relaxed Hair

Hair Classification   NT-12

Desired Color	Pre-Lightening Necessary	Product Category	Notes
Blondes			
Light Blonde Level 9	20vol / pwdr/ 2"	Demi 10g+ 10bv	Do not exceed over 10 mins/demi
Med. Blonde Level 7-8	20vol/pwdr/l Ligthnr crem 5inches	Demi 8g+10n	10n helps/ tone hair to soft blond /no
Dark Blonde Level 6	N/R	6bv +6g+1pt xtra lightnrcreme+ 25vol.	Add 1/3 part 6g to formula
Reds			
Light Red Level 7-8-9	10vl pwdr/ 2" Lt Creme	Demi 10g+ rc 10vl	Use 10vl to deposit color /Demi
Med. Red Level 5-6	N/R	6g+rc +1pt xlc 25vol	Add 1pt xlc for added lift to red orange
Dark Red Level 3-4	N/R	4ro + 1/3rc+ 25vol	Creates longer lasting reds
Brunettes			
Light Brown Level 5-6	N/R	10n +2inches grc + 25vol	Add 1/2 xlc /GrC to control warmth
Med. Brown Level 4-5	N/R	8n+1/4 lightnr crème 25vol	8n control warmth; lightener crème
Dark Brown Level 2-3	N/R	4g+ 25vol	20vol to create warm Dark brown

Copyright © 2007-2014 by David Velasco: All Rights Reserved : www.Haircolortradesecrets.com

Coloring African American Natural and Chemically Relaxed Hair

Hair Classification   NT-13

Desired Color	Pre-Lightening Necessary	Product Category	Notes
Blondes			
Light Blonde Level 9	20vl/pwdr/ 2' lightenrcreme	Demi 10g+ 10bv	Do not exceed 10mins
Med. Blonde Level 7-8	20vol/pwdr/crem lightner 5"	Demi 8g+10n	1/3pt10n helps/ tone hair to soft blonde
Dark Blonde Level 6	N/R	6bv+6g+ 1pt xtraligthnr 25vol.	25 vol for coarser hair 20 vol for finer texture
Reds			
Light Red Level 7-8-9	10vl pwdr/ 2inches lightning crème	Demi 10g+ rc 10vl	Use 10vol for demi no lift tone only.
Med. Red Level 5-6	N/R	6g+rc + xlc lightner+ 25vol	Add xlc 1 exta added lift
Dark Red Level 3-4	N/R	4ro + rc 25vol	1/3 rc creates longer lasting red tone.
Brunettes			
Light Brown Level 5-6	N/R	10n + 3"grc + 25vol	Add ¼pt lightr crème for added lift
Med. Brown Level 4-5	N/R	8n+ 25vol	8n controls warmth
Dark Brown Level 2-3	N/R	4g + 20vol	20vol for lift create warm pigment & deposit for richer color

Copyright © 2007-2014 by David Velasco: All Rights Reserved : www.Haircolortradesecrets.com

Coloring African American Natural and Chemically Relaxed Hair

Hair Classification   NT-14

Desired Color	Pre-Lightening Necessary	Product Category	Notes
Blondes			
Light Blonde Level 9	N/R	N/R	N/R
Med. Blonde Level 7-8	N/R	N/R	N/R
Dark Blonde Level 6	N/R	N/R	N/R
Reds			
Light Red Level 7-8-9	N/R	N/R	N/R
Med. Red Level 5-6	N/R	N/R	N/R
Dark Red Level 3-4	N/R	4ro + rc +10vol	Add rc for deeper hue of red tone/porosity issues
Brunettes			
Light Brown Level 5-6	N/R	N/R	N/R
Med. Brown Level 4-5	N/R	N/R	N/R
Dark Brown Level 2-3	N/R	4g/1/3pt gc + 10vol	keep vol at 10 /porosity issues

Copyright © 2007-2014 by David Velasco: All Rights Reserved : www.Haircolortradesecrets.com

Coloring African American Natural and Chemically Relaxed Hair

Hair Classification   NT-15

Desired Color	Pre-Lightening Necessary	Product Category	Notes
Blondes			
Light Blonde Level 9	N/R	N/R	Treatment / reshape hair damage
Med. Blonde Level 7-8	N/R	N/R	Treatment / reshape hair damage
Dark Blonde Level 6	N/R	N/R	Treatment / reshape hair damage
Reds			
Light Red Level 7-8-9		N/R	Treatment / reshape hair damage
Med. Red Level 5-6	N/R	N/R	Treatment / reshape hair damage
Dark Red Level 3-4	N/R	Semi-color red with gold base	Keep formula warm so the ends won't turn dark
Brunettes			
Light Brown Level 5-6	N/R	N/R	Treatment / reshape hair damage
Med. Brown Level 4-5	N/R	N/R	Treatment / reshape hair damage
Dark Brown Level 2-3	N/R	Semi-color brown with warm base	Use warm base /because hair is over-porous

Coloring African American Natural and Chemically Relaxed Hair

Group 2 – Chemically Relaxed Texture Charts

African American Chemically Relaxed Texture Chart

Slower ← → Faster

Milder ← No-Lye & Lye Relaxers → Stronger

		Thio Relaxers	Mild - Regular - Super	
Stages of Porosity	KEY	Ammonium Thioglycolate	"No-Lye" Hydroxide Relaxers	"Lye" Sodium Hydroxide
	Stage 1	CR-1	CR-6	CR-11
	Stage 2	CR-2	CR-7	CR-12
	Stage 3	CR-3	CR-8	CR-13
	Stage 4	CR-4	CR-9	CR-14
	Stage 5	CR-5	CR-10	CR-15

Mild - Regular - Super

Coloring African American Natural and Chemically Relaxed Hair

Hair Classification   CR-1

Desired Color	Pre-Lightening Necessary	Product Category	Notes
Blondes			
Light Blonde Level 9	N/R	N/R	N/R
Med. Blonde Level 7-8	N/R	N/R	N/R
Dark Blonde Level 6	N/R	N/R	N/R
Reds			
Light Red Level 7-8-9	N/R	N/R	N/R
Med. Red Level 5-6	N/R	N/R	N/R
Dark Red Level 3-4	N/R	N/R	N/R
Brunettes			
Light Brown Level 5-6	N/R	N/R	N/R
Med. Brown Level 4-5	N/R	N/R	N/R
Dark Brown Level 2-3	N/R	N/R	N/R

Copyright © 2007-2014 by David Velasco: All Rights Reserved : www.HaircolortradeSecrets.com

Coloring African American Natural and Chemically Relaxed Hair

Hair Classification   CR-2

Desired Color	Pre-Lightening Necessary	Product Category	Notes
Blondes			
Light Blonde Level 9	N/R	N/R	N/R
Med. Blonde Level 7-8	N/R	N/R	N/R
Dark Blonde Level 6	N/R	N/R	N/R
Reds			
Light Red Level 7-8-9	N/R	N/R	N/R
Med. Red Level 5-6	N/R	6ro + rc+ 1/2pt. xlc lighthr + 20vol	Adj amt of crème lightener on density and texture
Dark Red Level 3-4	N/R	4ro+ rc +20vl	Equal Parts will make a strong Dk Red tone.
Brunettes			
Light Brown Level 5-6	N/R	6bv+8"6g+1/2Pt xlc ligthnr+20vl	Using lightnr crème avoids using higher developer
Med. Brown Level 4-5	N/R	4g +1/2Pt.lightnr crème 20vol.	Hair is porous don't use high vol developer
Dark Brown Level 2-3	N/R	Demi 4g+ 20vol	20 vol & demi for slight Lift rich deposit

Coloring African American Natural and Chemically Relaxed Hair

Hair Classification   CR-3

Desired Color	Pre-Lightening Necessary	Product Category	Notes
Blondes			
Light Blonde Level 9	N/R	N/R	N/R
Med. Blonde Level 7-8	N/R	N/R	N/R
Dark Blonde Level 6	N/R	N/R	N/R
Reds			
Light Red Level 7-8-9	N/R	N/R	N/R
Med. Red Level 5-6	N/R	6ro + rc+ 1/2pt. xlc lighthr + 20vol	Adj amt of crème lightener on density and texture
Dark Red Level 3-4	N/R	4ro+ rc +20vl	Equal Parts will make a strong Bk Red tone.
Brunettes			
Light Brown Level 5-6	N/R	6bv+8"6g+1/2Pt xlc ligthnr+20vl	Using lightnr crème avoids using higher developer
Med. Brown Level 4-5	N/R	4g +1/2Pt.lightnr crème 20vol.	Hair is porous don't use high vol developer
Dark Brown Level 2-3	N/R	Demi 4g+ 20vol	20vl& Demi for slight Lift rich deposit

Coloring African American Natural and Chemically Relaxed Hair

Hair Classification   CR-4

Desired Color	Pre-Lightening Necessary	Product Category	Notes
Blondes			
Light Blonde Level 9	N/R	N/R	Nr/treatment/reshape hair if needed.
Med. Blonde Level 7-8	N/R	N/R	Nr/treatment/reshape hair if needed
Dark Blonde Level 6	N/R	N/R	Nr/treatment/reshape hair if needed.
Reds			
Light Red Level 7-8-9	N/R	N/R	Nr/treatment/reshape hair if needed.
Med. Red Level 5-6	N/R	N/R	Nr/treatment/reshape hair if needed.
Dark Red Level 3-4	N/R	Demi4ro+rc+10vl	Deep rich mahogany color
Brunettes			
Light Brown Level 5-6	N/R	N/R	Nr/treatment /reshape hair if needed
Med. Brown Level 4-5	N/R	N/R	Nr/treatment /reshape hair if needed
Dark Brown Level 2-3	N/R	Demi4g+ 1/3 pt gc 10vl	Use Demi for porosity issues

Coloring African American Natural and Chemically Relaxed Hair

Hair Classification   CR-5

Desired Color	Pre-Lightening Necessary	Product Category	Notes
Blondes			
Light Blonde Level 9	N/R	N/R	Nr/treatment/reshape hair if needed.
Med. Blonde Level 7-8	N/R	N/R	Nr/treatment/reshape hair if needed
Dark Blonde Level 6	N/R	N/R	Nr/treatment/reshape hair if needed.
Reds			
Light Red Level 7-8-9	N/R	N/R	Nr/treatment/reshape hair if needed.
Med. Red Level 5-6	N/R	N/R	Nr/treatment/reshape hair if needed.
Dark Red Level 3-4	N/R	Semi color red	keep gold base so the ends won't turn
Brunettes			
Light Brown Level 5-6	N/R	N/R	Nr/treatment/reshape hair if
Med. Brown Level 4-5	N/R	N/R	Nr/treatment/reshape hair if
Dark Brown Level 2-3	N/R	Semi honey brown	use semi for porosity issues

Coloring African American Natural and Chemically Relaxed Hair

Hair Classification CR-6

Desired Color	Pre-Lightening Necessary	Product Category	Notes
Blondes			
Light Blonde Level 9	N/R	N/R	N/R
Med. Blonde Level 7-8	N/R	N/R	N/R
Dark Blonde Level 6	N/R	N/R	N/R
Reds			
Light Red Level 7-8-9	N/R	N/R	N/R
Med. Red Level 5-6	N/R	N/R	N/R
Dark Red Level 3-4	N/R	N/R	N/R
Brunettes			
Light Brown Level 5-6	N/R	N/R	N/R
Med. Brown Level 4-5	N/R	N/R	N/R
Dark Brown Level 2-3	N/R	N/R	N/R

Copyright © 2007-2014 by David Velasco: All Rights Reserved : www.Haircolortradesecrets.com

Coloring African American Natural and Chemically Relaxed Hair

Hair Classification   CR-7

Desired Color	Pre-Lightening Necessary	Product Category	Notes
Blondes			
Light Blonde Level 9	pwdr/ 3" crème/10vl.	6 bv+6g+1Ptlightnr 25vl base/demi+10g/10bv	Do not exceed more than 10mins demi
Med. Blonde Level 7-8	pwdr/licrèm 5" 10vol	6 bv+1/3 pt.6g+ 20vl Demi10g+5" 10n	Add 1/3xlc to 6bv/6g/tone hilites
Dark Blonde Level 6	N/R	10g +6bv+1/2Pt. lightener crème +20	20vol for fine text/ 25 for coarser
Reds			
Light Red Level 7-8-9	pwdr/5"ligtrcrèm/ 10vl	rc +6ro+1 Pt.lighrcrem 20vol/demi8g+rc+10vl	Hilite over rc/6ro,tone demi
Med.Red Level 5-6	N/R	rc+ 6r+1Pt/lightning crème,20vol	Lightnr crem creates the added lift
Dark Red Level 3-4	N/R	4ro + red concentrate 20vol	20vl creates red orange lasting red
Brunettes			
Light Brown Level 5-6	N/R	6bv +1pt lightener crème 20vol	xlc gives need lift with no higher dev
Med. Brown Level 4-5	N/R	6bv +1/2 lightener crème 20 vol	Add lightener crème For added lift
Dark Brown Level 2-3	N/R	3n +1/3 gc. +20vol	Add gold cont no added developer

Coloring African American Natural and Chemically Relaxed Hair

Hair Classification   CR-8

Desired Color	Pre-Lightening Necessary	Product Category	Notes
Blondes			
Light Blonde Level 9	pwdr/ 3"crème/10vl.	Base 6 bv+6g+1pt lightener crème 25 vol	Demi+10g/10bv tone hilites 10mins or
Med. Blonde Level 7-8	pwdr/ 5"lightnrcrem 10vol	6 bv+1/3 pt.6g+ 1/2Ptlightnr crem 25vl	Demi +10g+5"10n /tone hilites
Dark Blonde Level 6	Pwdr/5"lightnr Crème	10g +6bv+1/2Pt. lightener crème +20	Tone Demi 6g 10vl
Reds			20vol for fine text/ 25 for coarser
Light Red Level 7-8-9	pwdr/crème/10vl	Base rc +6ro+1pt crème dev 20vol/	Tone hilites /demi 8g+rc+10vl
Med.Red Level 5-6	N/R	rc+ 6r+1Pt/lightning crème,20vol	Crème lightnr adds lift to red orange
Dark Red Level 3-4	N/R	4ro + red concentrate 20vol	20vol creates right amt underpigment
Brunettes			
Light Brown Level 5-6	N/R	6bv +1pt lightener crème 2ovol	Lightener crème gives higher lift
Med. Brown Level 4-5	N/R	6bv + 1/2ligthnr crème 20 vol	Lightener crème creates mor warmth
Dark Brown Level 2-3	N/R	3n +1/3 gc +20vol	Add gold cont no added developer

Coloring African American Natural and Chemically Relaxed Hair

Hair Classification CR-9

Desired Color	Pre-Lightening Necessary	Product Category	Notes
Blondes			
Light Blonde Level 9	N/R	N/R	N/R
Med. Blonde Level 7-8	N/R	N/R	N/R
Dark Blonde Level 6	N/R	N/R	N/R
Reds			
Light Red Level 7-8-9	N/R	N/R	N/R
Med. Red Level 5-6	N/R	N/R	N/R
Dark Red Level 3-4	N/R	4ro + 1/3pt rc 10vol	Keep formula warm for porosity issues
Brunettes			
Light Brown Level 5-6	N/R	N/R	N/R
Med. Brown Level 4-5	N/R	N/R	N/R
Dark Brown Level 2-3	N/R	4g +1/3 pt gc +10vol	Add gold concentrate no added developer

Coloring African American Natural and Chemically Relaxed Hair

Hair Classification   CR-10

Desired Color	Pre-Lightening Necessary	Product Category	Notes
Blondes			
Light Blonde Level 9	N/R	N/R	Nr/treatment/reshape hair if needed.
Med. Blonde Level 7-8	N/R	N/R	Nr/treatment/reshape hair if needed
Dark Blonde Level 6	N/R	N/R	Nr/treatment/reshape hair if needed.
Reds			
Light Red Level 7-8-9	N/R	N/R	Nr/treatment/reshape hair if needed.
Med. Red Level 5-6	N/R	N/R	Nr/treatment/reshape hair if needed.
Dark Red Level 3-4	N/R	Semi color red	Keep gold base so the ends won't turn dark
Brunettes			
Light Brown Level 5-6	N/R	N/R	Nr/treatment /reshape hair if needed
Med. Brown Level 4-5	N/R	N/R	Nr/treatment /reshape hair if needed
Dark Brown Level 2-3	N/R	Semi color honey brown	Keep semi warm /porous hair

Copyright © 2007-2014 by David Velasco: All Rights Reserved : www.Haircolortradesecrets.com

Coloring African American Natural and Chemically Relaxed Hair

Hair Classification   CR-11

Desired Color	Pre-Lightening Necessary	Product Category	Notes
Blondes			
Light Blonde Level 9	N/R	N/R	N/R
Med. Blonde Level 7-8	N/R	N/R	N/R
Dark Blonde Level 6	N/R	N/R	N/R
Reds			
Light Red Level 7-8-9	N/R	N/R	N/R
Med. Red Level 5-6	N/R	N/R	N/R
Dark Red Level 3-4	N/R	N/R	N/R
Brunettes			
Light Brown Level 5-6	N/R	N/R	N/R
Med. Brown Level 4-5	N/R	N/R	N/R
Dark Brown Level 2-3	N/R	N/R	N/R

Coloring African American Natural and Chemically Relaxed Hair

Hair Classification   CR-12

Desired Color	Pre-Lightening Necessary	Product Category	Notes
Blondes			Add 25 vol for coarser hair
Light Blonde Level 9	Pwdr/3"lightnrcrème 10vol	6 bv+1/3Pt8g+1/2Pt xlightnrcreme20Vl	Tone hilites / Demi 10g+10vl/10 mins or less
Med. Blonde Level 7-8	pwdr/5" lighteningcrème 10vol	6 bv+ 1/3 Pt8g+ 1/2Pt xtralightnr creme 20vl	Tone hilites / 10g/5"10n 10vl
Dark Blonde Level 6	pwdr/5 inches lightener crème 10vol	6bv+1pt lightener creme+20vl /demi6g	Color base to level5 than hilite over light Brn base
Reds			Add 25 vl for coarser hair
Light Red Level 7-8-9	pwdr/3" lightnr crème/10vl	rc +6ro+1/2pt xlc Lightener crème 20vol	Tone hilites demi/ 8g+1/3Pt rc+10vl
Med. Red Level 5-6	N/R	rc+ 6ro +1Pt. Lightnrcreme 20vol	Lightnr crème add lift/without high dev
Dark Red Level 3-4	N/R	4ro + red concentrate 20vol	Rc creates rich vibrant red
Brunettes			Use 25 vol for coarser hair
Light Brown Level 5-6	N/R	6bv+1/3Pt 6g1,Pt Lightener crème 20vol	Lighnr crème gives added lift
Med. Brown Level 4-5	N/R	6bv +1/3 Pt6g, 1/2Pt Lightening crème 20 vol	6bv controls brassy warm tone
Dark Brown Level 2-3	N/R	3n+1/3pt 4g + 20vol	4g adds rich tonality

Coloring African American Natural and Chemically Relaxed Hair

Hair Classification   CR-13

Desired Color	Pre-Lightening Necessary	Product Category	Notes
Blondes			
Light Blonde Level 9	Scoop Pwdr/ 5"lightneing Crème 10vol	6 bv+1/3Pt8g+1Pt xlightening crème 20vol Demi +10g+10vl	Tone Hilites/ Demi10g+10vl/ 10mins or less
Med. Blonde Level 7-8	Scoop pwdr/3 " lightening crème 10vol	6 bv+ 1/3 Pt8g+ 1Pt xtralightnr crème 20vl	Tone hilites demi 10g/10vl .5" no added dev
Dark Blonde Level 6	Scoop/pwdr/3" lightening crème 10vol	6bv+1pt lightener creme+20vl /demi6g 10g	Color base to level5 than hilite over light Brn base
Reds			
Light Red Level 7-8-9	Scoop pwdr/3" lightener crème/10vl	rc +6ro+1 Pt lightener crème 20vol/demi 8g+1/3Ptrc+10vl	Tone hilites / demi 8g+1/3Pt rc+10vl
Med.Red Level 5-6	N/R	rc+ 6ro +1/2Pt. Lightener crème 20vl	Lightener crème add lift/without high dev
Dark Red Level 3-4	N/R	4ro + red concentrate 20vol	Rc creates rich vibrant red
Brunettes			
Light Brown Level 5-6	N/R	6bv+1/3Pt 6g1,Pt Lightener crème 20vol	Lightener crème gives added lift
Med. Brown Level 4-5	N/R	6bv +1/3 Pt6g, 1/2Pt Lightening crème 20 vol	6bv controls brassy warm tone
Dark Brown Level 2-3	N/R	3n+1/3pt 4g + 20vol	4g adds rich tonality

Coloring African American Natural and Chemically Relaxed Hair

Hair Classification   CR-14

Desired Color	Pre-Lightening Necessary	Product Category	Notes
Blondes			
Light Blonde Level 9	N/R	N/R	Nr/treatment/reshape hair if needed.
Med. Blonde Level 7-8	N/R	N/R	Nr/treatment/reshape hair if needed
Dark Blonde Level 6	N/R	N/R	Nr/treatment/reshape hair if needed.
Reds			
Light Red Level 7-8-9	N/R	N/R	Nr/treatment/reshape hair if needed.
Med. Red Level 5-6	N/R	N/R	Nr/treatment/reshape hair if needed.
Dark Red Level 3-4	N/R	Semi color red	Keep gold base so the ends won't turn dark
Brunettes			
Light Brown Level 5-6	N/R	N/R	Nr/treatment /reshape hair if needed
Med. Brown Level 4-5	N/R	N/R	Nr/treatment /reshape hair if needed
Dark Brown Level 2-3	N/R	Semi Honey Brn	Keep semi warm /porous grab Drk

Coloring African American Natural and Chemically Relaxed Hair

Hair Classification   CR-15

Desired Color	Pre-Lightening Necessary	Product Category	Notes
Blondes			
Light Blonde Level 9	N/R	N/R	Nr/treatment/reshape hair if needed.
Med. Blonde Level 7-8	N/R	N/R	Nr/treatment/reshape hair if needed
Dark Blonde Level 6	N/R	N/R	Nr/treatment/reshape hair if needed.
Reds			
Light Red Level 7-8-9	N/R	N/R	Nr/treatment/reshape hair if needed.
Med. Red Level 5-6	N/R	N/R	Nr/treatment/reshape hair if needed.
Dark Red Level 3-4	N/R	Semi color red	Keep gold base so the ends won't turn dark
Brunettes			
Light Brown Level 5-6	N/R	N/R	Nr/treatment/reshape hair if needed
Med. Brown Level 4-5	N/R	N/R	Nr/treatment/reshape hair if needed
Dark Brown Level 2-3	N/R	Semi Honey Brn	Keep semi warm/porous hair

Coloring African American Natural and Chemically Relaxed Hair

After Care ---- Hair Care Products

We discussed earlier that hair porosity reveals the condition of the hair and is acutely related to elasticity allowing the hair to stretch and return without breaking.

The cortex within the hair strand, which makes up most of the physical properties (strength, elasticity) must be in good condition. So a healthy head of hair must have a combination of controlled normal porosity, good elasticity and a healthy cuticle.

When applying relaxers and permanent color to the hair it not only raises the cuticle but also affects the cortex which will ultimately alter the elasticity of the hair strands. The more heat that is applied, through the use of heating implements or chemicals, the more loss in elasticity occurs, triggering abnormal porosity and a damage cortex.

This is where hair begins to become dry and brittle, and void of moisture. This is because it has cracks and breaks in the hair shaft, which makes the hair susceptible to breakage when stretched, combed or styled.

As licensed professionals, we should be knowledgeable in advising all our clients on the best hair care and treatments for their hair. How we do that is by being knowledgeable in understanding hair texture, porosity, elasticity and how we can avoid damaging the cuticle. This knowledge assists the colorist in knowing what type of condition the hair is in and therefore what product selection needs to be done before the color begins.

Choosing the right products goes far beyond price, feel and smell. Generally speaking, color and relaxers are incompatible if one doesn't know how to control the pH balance by selecting products that can reduce the high alkaline chemical application back into an acidic environment.

This is why it is critical to have professional hair care lines that not only reinforce the cuticle layer of the hair shaft but also protect relaxed or texture hair from permanent color or heated styling implements.

pH Balance

We wrote earlier about importance of knowing the pH scale and how it relates to the products we use. However, we would like to briefly talk to you from a stylist point of view about how to use the pH scale when it comes to choosing the right hair care products for specific hair textures you are servicing.

Healthy hair has a pH of between 4 and 6. Many hair care products have so many synthetic ingredients that it is ridiculous! We often, as stylists, rate our product use based on how our hair feels not having any idea that our hair feeling soft and smooth may only be because the product that we use coated our hair strands with synthetic fillers. The pH of hair products is one of the least examined but most important characteristics of hair care products.

Shampoos and conditioners that have synthetic ingredients will make our hair initially feel soft, but in turn will dry out the hair by leaving the hair cuticle too open and susceptible to the natural elements in the air, which is a common problem among virgin and relaxed hair.

Coloring African American Natural and Chemically Relaxed Hair

This is where dryness and breakage usually occur because the hair is not within the proper pH range. This is of great importance when working on Afro Caribbean hair that has been colored or chemically relaxed or both!

Afro textured hair has its own requirements when it comes to selecting shampoos and conditioners that are best suited for that hair type. The best shampoos for textured hair are acidic, with a pH of less than 7, usually between a pH of 4.5 to 5.5, so the hair is cleansed but not stripped of its natural oils or moisture.

Product Bar:

Shampoos

Afro textured hair tends to be less oily than other hair types because of the tightness of the curl pattern, which prevents the natural sebum (oil) from flowing down the full length of the hair shaft.

The shampoos used should be moisturizing to the scalp but strong enough to remove dirt and oils and other product buildup leaving the hair manageable and tangle free.

Sulfate free shampoos work great on texture hair depositing moisture and nutrients where needed in the dry porous areas of the hair.

Ingredients to look for in a shampoo are:

- Sodium Lauroyl Glutamate
- Sodium Myristoyl Glutamate
- Sodium Cocoyl Sarcosinate
- Sodium Myristoyl Sarcosinate
- Oleoyl Sarcosinehampoo's

The moisturizing properties in these ingredients impact textured hair improving manageability and smoothness to the cuticle layers of the hair.

Conditioners

The fragileness of textured hair presents specific needs that require conditioning properties that address constant dryness from chemicals. New technology has imparted moisture retention proteins that not only strengthen hair for elasticity but also dramatically improve porosity and shine.

Ingredients to look for in choosing good conditioners are:

- Hydrolyzed Wheat Protein
- Hydrolyzed Soy protein
- Hydrolyzed keratin protein
- And Keravis

Coloring African American Natural and Chemically Relaxed Hair

Conditioners formulated with these ingredients have "strengthening complex" that penetrates beyond the cuticle layer into the cortex to dramatically improve the condition of damaged or chemically depended hair.

Leave-in Conditioner

Hair is constantly exposed to elements such as the sun, heating tools and chlorine, leaving the hair feeling dry, frizzy and brittle by opening up the cuticle layers .Leave-in conditioners assist in keeping a low porosity levels so the cuticle remains sealed.

This sets the stage for   blow-drying and styling.

Ingredients to look for are

- Essential oils
- Vitamins
- Amino acids

And moisturizing proteins such as

- Sunflower oil
- Biotin
- Hydrolyzed soy protein
- Wheat germ oil
- And castor oil

Shine Serum

Shine Serums should be lightweight and non-greasy to use for shinning, calming frizz and using for flat iron work.

Recently silicone agents in hair products have received both negative and positive reviews pertaining to Afro textured hair. The key factor in knowing what type of silicone serum to use is to determine if it is non-water soluble which creates build up or water soluble which makes it easy shampoo out.

Note: This is why prewashing a new guest with a clarifying shampoo is recommended. This will get rid of all past product residues including silicone buildup before you perform your color service, so your color will have better penetration and take more evenly.

As you know there is a huge inventory of shine serums in our industry to choose from; however, the silicones you want to steer away from are the non-water soluble silicones.

The Most Important Ingredients to watch for are: (not an exhaustive list)

- Cetearyl Methicone
- Cetyl Dimethicone

Coloring African American Natural and Chemically Relaxed Hair

- Dimethicone
- Stearyl Dimethicone

The water-soluble silicones you want to use for your clients are:

- Dimethicone Copolyol
- Lauryl Methicone Copolyol
- or any ingredient with "Peg" as a prefix.

It's that simple, once you have decided which water-soluble silicones products to use; your next step is to make sure your product has one of the many essential oils and vitamins in your serum.

Such as

- Linseed oil
- Wheat germ oil
- Argon oil
- Vitamin E
- Pomegranate oil

All of these ingredients should be molecularly structured to be lightweight and can be applied to almost any texture you service in your salon.

Shine Mist

Shine Mist provide protection for color treated hair against Uva /Uvb rays. The product shouldn't have any alcohol or water in it. A good shine mist works well with flat irons and leaves no greasy residue on the iron while creating a beautiful finishing shine on most textures.

As we stated earlier, the cuticle layer of the hair operates like a vent, it lifts and then it lowers (actually it swells and lowers) depending on the type of products you use.

For many decades mineral oil and petroleum-based products were specifically designed for Afro textured hair to create a high, glossy finish, but it only stayed on top of the hair shaft allowing no moisture to get into the hair!

Today our industry has evolved giving the stylist better choices in selecting essential oils over petroleum and mineral oil based products.

The difference between an essential oil, mineral oil and petroleum oil is that essential oils can permeate the hair and diffuse, thus allowing the hair to take in moisture. Mineral and petroleum-based products CANNOT do this!

Essential oils provide many more benefits when compared to mineral oil products. They encourage hair growth, help alleviate dry hair and scalp and are beneficial for helping eliminating dandruff and an itchy scalp.

Coloring African American Natural and Chemically Relaxed Hair

Today's market has greatly expanded in the use of essential oils and some manufacturers have also created crème based leave-in conditioners infused with essential oils. These products have proven to be very beneficial for Afro texture hair.

This is not an exhaustive list but the ingredients to look for in an essential oil or crème based leave in products are:

- Rosemary
- Sage
- Olive oil
- Jojoba oil
- Lavender

Each of these ingredients has a specific benefit in promoting healthy scalp and hair.

Coloring African American Natural and Chemically Relaxed Hair

After Care Retailing

Retailing to your clients is not an option, it is a necessity! This will support the work of you color services.

Your retailing success will depend on how well you communicate to your client's needs and the benefits and features of your products .

<u>Some general guidelines for after-care are for clients :</u>

- Heat can be your friend if you can control it or your foe if you don't. Constant flat iron use on color treated hair or relaxed hair will produce color fading, dehydration, brittleness and breakage. Only use the flat iron on a warm setting twice a week.

- Wait 48 hrs. Before shampooing hair when client has received a color service.

- Use wide comb with rounded teeth or wet detangling brush when detangling hair after shampooing.

- Shampoo hair at home with sulfate free shampoo with no parabens or sodium chloride.

- For virgin, chemically relaxed hair or color treated hair, use a deep conditioner once a month to maintain the hair's integrity and moisture balance, allowing it to withstand regular manipulation and styling, as well as preventing damage.

- When sleeping at night use satin pillow case or wear satin bonnet or silk scarves to maintain moisture in hair!

- Use daily crème moisture based product with essential oils for relaxed hair or virgin hair.

- Use daily essential oils for the ends of the hair shaft for natural hair or relaxed hair depending on texture.

- **<u>Do NOT</u>** use the pressing comb on chemically processed hair. Pressing combs were not intended for chemically processed hair. Instead use a warm ionic flat iron.

- **Do NOT** over brush hair. Despite the common myth that 100 strokes a day are good for the hair and scalp, this leads to breakage!!

- Little brushing as possible, the kinkier the hair the less you should brush.

- When a client is transitioning to braids or weaves to give her hair a rest, DO NOT RELAX HER HAIR. No need to relax hair because she will need the strength of her new growth in getting braids or the added weight of weaves.

Coloring African American Natural and Chemically Relaxed Hair

- Avoid applying grease, mineral oils or petroleum oils on the scalp for itching or flaking, it will clog up the hair follicle, repel moisture from the hair and slows down hair growth.

- Do not wear braids too tightly as they can cause traction alopecia, which is just one of the many leading causes of hair loss among African American women!

- Don't over wrap hair as it can thin it out and cause breakage at the hair line.

- Alternate styling technique at night using medium size pin curls which adds more body to the hair or if hair is relaxed, use rollers in the morning.

- Put shower cap over the hair and the steam of the shower will form a curl. This way you can avoid using a flat iron every morning to create volume in your hair.

Summary

Hair care and after care is what keeps clients in your salon and your chair!

One of the most common problems that is constant for colorists is combating against the dryness of Afro Caribbean hair. However this does not have to be a struggle. It starts with understanding the pH scale and being knowledgeable in hair care ingredients that the manufacturers use to formulate their products.

Understanding this will not allow you to be misled by marketing campaigns or by companies trying to sell you the wrong products for your clients.

The golden rule I use that was passed along to me many years ago by a distributor is:

"He or she that can control the pH levels that fluxuate during the processing of chemical relaxers and hair coloring will build a successful business in coloring texture hair! "

It's that simple to hearing it, but it takes training, experience and mentoring to develop.

After care is a very important service to deliver at your salon.

Clients today with social media, along with access to so-called expert pundits blogs who are not licensed professionals, will leave the salon BECAUSE THEY FEEL YOU CAN'T TAKE CARE OF THEIR NEEDS.

They will find someone who can or try to do their own color or relaxer at home, along with creating their own hair care regime.

So we as industry professionals must take time to educate and teach our clients what we use and what they need to take home for use, so it becomes a win, win situation for both you and your guest.

Coloring African American Natural and Chemically Relaxed Hair

At Home After-Care Maintenance Tips

Having chemically relaxed and color treated hair requires more home-care maintenance in order to keep hair color from quickly fading and to maintain the moisture balance needed for body, shine and movement.

The following are some general rules that are recommend to clients:

1. Don't wash your hair for at least 48 hour's after the hair has been colored. Allow the color to settle within the hair shaft.

2. Avoid hot water. It dries out the hair and scalp causing the haircolor to fade prematurely. Warm water is sufficient to shampoo hair and cool water to rinse hair. This helps to not only keep the color but also maintain the integrity of the hair and shine.

3. Use Sulfate free shampoo, rich in moisture to avoid excessive dryness, tangling and knotting on the ends of the hair.

4. Conditioners should be formulated with moisturizing proteins that lock into the hair shaft for strength and helps to repair a degree of damage sustained from chemical service.

5. Liquid moisturizing treatments provided once a month are great to prevent hair from getting over porous and loose elasticity caused by a continuation of multiple chemical services.

6. Essential oil products can and should be used on dense, excessively curly and kinky textures to seal in moisture. Mineral oils, petroleums are to be avoided .

7. Clients should be using a light-weight leave-in conditioner, they can be applied every day for curly and kinky textures to maintain optimum moisture levels within the hair.

8. Satin bonnets, silk scarves and satin pillowcases are a necessity for clients to take home because it keeps the pH level of moisture consistent. Cotton, wool and other fabric's draw away moisture from the hair.

Coloring African American Natural and Chemically Relaxed Hair

9. During the winter months guide your clients away from wearing hat and wool scarves that don't have satin or silk linings. They will be able to avoid breakage and keep moisture in their hair even during the winter months.

10. Heat should be kept to a minimum. That has always been the culprit in causing hair that is chemically treated or colored to become brittle, porous easy to break off because of a lack of restraint . It's the responsibility of the stylist to tell the client the importance of their recommendation.

11. When swimming, colored treated hair should be carefully protected by pre-wetting the hair then using a conditioner to create a barrier so that the chlorine does not absorb into the hair. Also a swim cap should be worn for maximum protection. This level of protection will help keep the cuticle from eroding away, resulting in dry porous ends or color fading and it will also help fight against the green cast that is caused by chlorine in the water.

Coloring African American Natural and Chemically Relaxed Hair

Other Haircolor Education Programs From David Velasco

HaircolorTradeSecrets.com
FREE Haircolor Ebook
Haircolor Books - Creative Foiling DVD's - Audio CD's
Trade Secrets of a Haircolor Expert — David Velasco

HaircolorClubhouse.com
FREE Haircolor VIDEOS
Network with Thousands of Hairdressers - Haircolor BLOGS - Haircolor Photos
The Haircolor Experts "Networking Club House" by David Velasco

HaircolorUniversity.com
12 Month - MultiMedia E-Course in the Art of Haircolor
Streaming and Downloadable - Videos - Audios - PDF
Haircolor *University* By David Velasco

Coloring African American Natural and Chemically Relaxed Hair

David Velasco "LIVE" Class DVD's

Available at:
HaircolorTradeSecrets.com

Haircolor Trade Secrets "LIVE" Class DVD's

- Haircolor 101 – The Beginning
- How Haircolor Really Works
- Gray Coverage Class
- Amazing Redheads Class
- Exotic Brunettes Class
- Single Process Blondes Blondes
- Double Process Blondes
- Color Correction Made Easy
- Color Correction for Redheads
- Color Correction for Blondes
- Color Correction for Gary Coverage
- 101 Haircolor Trade Secrets
- Men's Haircolor Secrets
- Coloring African-American Hair
- Haircolor Consultation Skills
- How to Become a Recognized Haircolor Expert
- How to Make More Money Behind The Chair
- The Ultimate Salon Marketing Plan

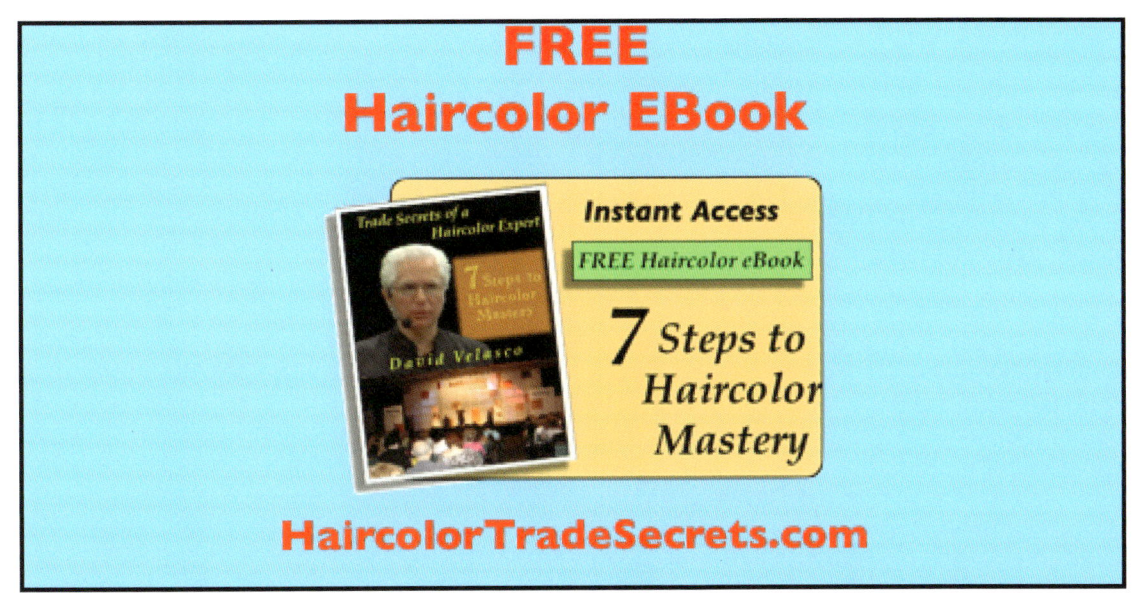

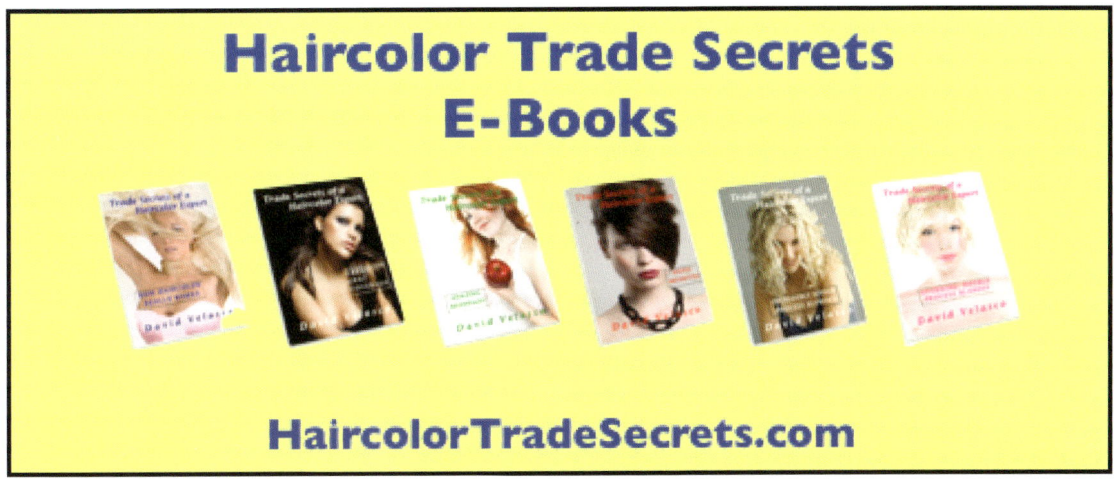

Coloring African American Natural and Chemically Relaxed Hair

FREE Haircolor EBook

7 Steps to Haircolor Mastery

HaircolorTradeSecrets.com

Haircolor Trade Secrets E-Books

HaircolorTradeSecrets.com

Haircolor Trade Secrets Audio Books

HaircolorTradeSecrets.com

Coloring African American Natural and Chemically Relaxed Hair

David Velasco

- *HAIRCOLOR SPECIALIST*
- *MASTER STYLIST*
- *SALON OWNER*
- *EDUCATOR*
- *CONSULTANT*
- *AUTHOR*

With 40 years Experience in the field of hairdressing, Velasco has become one of the industry's leading authorities.

Velasco began his career at the young age of 16 in Tampa.Fla. He soon moved to London, England where he worked and studied his craft with world-renowned hairdressers of that era.

Upon return to the USA Velasco began to develop his skills as an Educator and Effective Communicator while working with John & Suzzane Chadwick at the "Hair Fashion Development Center" on New York's 5th Ave.

By the age of 21 Velasco was STYLES DIRECTOR for the SAKS FIFTH AVE. beauty salon in New York City. Over the next 20 years Velasco became involved in almost every aspect of hair related activities possible. Including such achievements as, Freelance Hair Designer for photo sessions with major beauty publications and television commercials. He has held such prestige positions as Educational and Creative Consultant to CLAIROL INC., SHISEIDO LTD.,& THE WELLA CORP..

He has preformed as the Featured Guest Artist and Master Educator at hundreds of trade events throughout the world. His presentation at HAIRCOLOR U.S.A., symposium was rated BEST EDUCATIONAL EVENT by his peers.

Velasco has been a Contributing Author to many hair related articles for both consumer and professional publications and books. Velasco held a position as the NATIONAL ARTISTIC DIRECTOR FOR THE WELLA CORP. for ten years and is a member of the INTERNATIONAL HAIRCOLOR EXCHANGE.

Velasco was formally the DIRECTOR OF HAIRCOLOR for the world renowned BUMBLE & BUMBLE SALON in NEW YORK CITY and presently resides over his own salon David Velasco Salon, LTD. in Doylestown, Pennsylvania.

David and his Salon are proud members of INTERCOIFFURE MONDIAL, which is the most prestigious international hairdressing organization in the world.

As an industry leader, David is also owner of "Salon Success Systems Publications" through which he has Authored and Self-Published many books in the Art of Haircolor branded: **"Trade Secrets of a Haircolor Expert",** and produced a Series of Educational DVD's and a social networking website:**"The Haircolor Clubhouse"** where he provides free haircolor education to professional hairdressers around the world.

CPSIA information can be obtained at www.ICGtesting.com
Printed in the USA
LVIW01n1616060317
526285LV00011B/162